"The World's Greatest Project"

One Project Team on
the Path to Quality

"The World's Greatest Project"

One Project Team on the Path to Quality

Russell W. Darnall

A Project Management Institute Book

Project Management Institute
130 South State Road
Upper Darby, PA 19082
610/734-3330

Library of Congress Cataloging-in-Publication Data

Darnall, Russell W., 1950–
  "The world's greatest project": one project team on the path to quality/by Russell W. Darnall.
         p.   cm.
    ISBN: 1-880410-46-X   (pbk.)
      1. Total quality management.   2. Work groups.   3. Quality circles. I. Title.
    HD62.15.D37   1996
    658.5'62—dc20   95-36169
                                                        CIP

Book Team

Editor-in-Chief	*James S. Pennypacker*
Book Editor	*Jeannette Cabanis*
Associate Editor	*Sandy Jenkins*
Graphic Designer	*Michelle T. Owen*
Production Coordinator	*Mark S. Parker*
Publications Coordinator	*Bobby R. Hensley*
Proofreader	*Ann Wright*

Illustrations by *Randy Glasbergen*

PMI books are available at special quantity discounts to use as premiums and sales promotions, or for use in corporate training programs. For more information, please write to the Business Manager, PMI Communications, 40 Colonial Square, Sylva, NC 28779 USA or contact your local bookstore.

The paper used in this book complies with the Permanent Paper Standard issued by the National Information Standards Organization (Z39.48—1984).

10   9   8   7   6   5   4   3   2   1

Table of Contents

Foreword(s)

TOTAL QUALITY MANAGEMENT (TQM)—and particularly its application outside the manufacturing environment—is not a well-defined concept. Many service companies have adopted the concept in principle, gone through the rigors of extensive training, including pledges by senior management of support and commitment, only to find widespread failure.

The failures are not for lack of good intention, but rather stem from the inability to adapt TQM to the measurements of success in the service industry. Success is further compromised by a middle management attitude most often reflected by the "buzzword" syndrome, which inhibits them in fully understanding, supporting, and proactively practicing the latest management philosophy.

For those visionary individuals with challenges in front of them, this book should help chart their path.

The service business is mostly comprised of projects, each project for an individual client and each project led by a project manager of sorts. The opportunity exists for the project manager to develop a concept, culture and philosophy for each project.

The World's Greatest Project presents four basic concepts that are paramount to a successful project:

1. *Look for solutions, not blame.* The search for a solution too often either appears to point the finger or ends up doing so—a largely non-productive effort. Look for the solution.

2. *Goal-Directed.* The project team must have a common direction and measurable goal, so that achievement can be measured.

3. *Client-Focused.* How often have we heard that an objective was met, only to find out that that objective was not what the client really wanted?

4. *People-Oriented.* The service industry's primary resource is people. We must involve people not only in the successes but also the failures. We must, as managers, allow them and expect them to take ownership in their work, set high expectations, reward them when they succeed, and console them when they fail.

I strongly recommend this book to all project personnel in both the client and service-providing companies. The concepts work. They work on any project of any size but are most effective when the client and service company work together. *Goal-directed, client-focused, and people-oriented* are only "buzzwords" until they are understood and practiced. There is no magic formula; the project manager must tailor-make the program. The project manager must, however, first have an understanding of the client's needs and objectives; second, establish goals aimed at meeting those needs and objectives; and third, get commitment from the team to meet those goals and reward them when they do. If the program is reasonable, that "when" *will* happen.

Russ, in writing this book, has captured the essence of TQM for a project. I applaud his endurance and persistence on completing this book while simultaneously exceeding the expectations of the project team of which he was a part.

Bill Leistner
Manager of Operations, Ferrous Metals
Fluor Daniel

F OR THE PROFESSIONAL project manager, Russ Darnall has captured the essence of Total Quality Management as applied to project management in an extremely interesting, easy-to-understand manner.

As a professional project manager who has successfully used this approach, I feel that this information is the most important development to emerge in thirty years. Project managers, clients, customers, and stakeholders all need to understand the implications and importance of Total Quality Management for projects, including goal setting and the use of team efforts to achieve these goals.

Russ's approach will require a leap of faith by the progressive project manager who wants to improve, but—take it from one who has tried it—though it might seem like child's play at first, it will take shape and create success as the project proceeds. The project manager who tries this approach will be encouraged constantly by the entire team as they work together, self-measuring and meeting goals they have been involved in setting. He will find himself becoming a coach, clearing obstacles to the team's success. He might even have fun along the way. The end result will be total project success.

What more could a professional project manager ask for?

John R. Thatcher
Vice President of Project Management for Fluor Daniel, retired

Preface

SOMETHING MAGICAL OCCURS when a project team begins to align on common objectives, when the plan starts coming together, when the team generates a new and creative approach to an "insoluble" problem.

Something magical occurs when the client's dream starts taking shape in the form of the project plan, when the team celebrates that first milestone and when project success becomes a set of clear expectations.

Something magical occurs when every member of the team can identify how their contribution helps achieve the project goal.

Something magical happens on projects—and the magician is the project manager.

I've seen the magic and worked with some of the best magicians. Although there is a scientist in every project manager, it is the artist, the creator that makes the magic. This story is about that magic and some of the magician's tricks.

Since the first generation of this story, *Achieving TQM on Projects*, was published in 1994, I have supported projects in Asia and South America, developing a new understanding of the cultural aspects of the art of project management while reaffirming my understanding of other aspects. I have learned a few more of the magician's tricks and witnessed the excitement, the fun and yes, the magic of those special projects—the projects managed by the artist. I have also witnessed projects that became much less than they were capable of becoming, where work was tiring and almost painful. These, too, were learning experiences.

The World's Greatest Project contains my reflections on some of these new experiences. It is a continuation of the story I told in *Achieving TQM on Projects,* and more. The title change conveys more about the experiences and the pride of the team that experienced the events captured in the story.

Revising and expanding this book also gave me the opportunity to improve a completed project. How many project managers get that chance?

Russell W. Darnall
August, 1996

From the preface to
Achieving TQM on Projects

IN MEDICINE, the relationship of the surgeon to the general practitioner is similar to the relationship of the project manager to the general manager. While the general practitioner treats a patient from beginning to end, developing a long-term approach to health, the surgeon usually sees a patient to deal with a specific condition, then turns the patient back to the general practitioner.

Because of this special relationship with the patient, the surgeon must not only develop good general medical skills, but must develop special skills in his medical expertise. Because the time frame is much shorter, the surgeon must quickly develop the trust of the patient, must understand the unique needs of the patient, and must develop a plan that quickly deals with the problem. After the plan is executed, either successfully or unsuccessfully, the surgeon must discontinue the relationship and move on to the next case.

Project managers operate in much the same way. As a project manager, you manage a project that impacts the health of a larger organization, you have a time-limited task to complete, and then you move on to your next project. Just as the surgeon must develop special skills and techniques, the project manager develops skills and techniques that are critical for the job at hand. In both executing your tasks and in developing relationships with your patients, the skills you develop are somewhat different than those of the general practitioner.

Just as a surgeon watches for new developments in medicine that will have an impact on his or her specialty, project managers watch for developments in management that have an impact on project management. One development that has received a lot of attention from project managers is Total Quality Management (TQM). Many of the TQM practices developed for the manufacturing environment have some form of application on projects, some do not have any application, and some new applications have been developed that apply specifically on projects.

This book explores the developing expertise of applying TQM concepts to the project management environment.

Russell W. Darnall
December, 1993

Acknowledgements

O F ALL HUMAN RELATIONSHIPS, one of the most complex is that of boss-employee. In an era of economic transition, when the label "boss" has a negative connotation, I have been extremely fortunate in that I have worked with some of the best in the industry. Bosses who personify the ideal. People who teach and mentor, inspire and empower. Friends that you can trust and take risks with.

A special thanks to Steve MacLeod, who still supports the journey; Steve Gilbert, who made the transition easy; Marilyn Coll, who kept me connected although I was 6,000 miles away; and especially to Bill Leistner, who was critical to the development of this book. He nurtured the initial stages of development, provided the model for many of the chapters, and gave honest and helpful feedback. He continues to be a source of inspiration and strength. It is no coincidence that all these people are part of Fluor Daniel.

The understanding and managing of project complexity were concepts developed with my friend John Thatcher. They resulted in the Project Complexity Index discussed in Chapter 10.

My thanks also goes to the Alumbrera Project Team—a project and a team that provided the wealth of learning experiences.

The learning continues with my new teammates: Tex Carter and Cesare Celle in Chile, Gary Davis in Argentina, Americo Bortollozo in Brazil, and Rick Anaya in Peru.

A number of friends and coworkers have helped make South America a home as well as an adventure: Phil and Vicky Chicola, Orlando Lopez, Marshall Evans, Tony and Joyce Maycock, Paulo Bertamini, Antonio Plaza, Lloyd Warren, Mario Marcheese, Mike and Donna Freeze, Tawna Hill and definitely not last nor least, Dezi MacLeod.

When you are 6,000 miles from home the term "long-time friend" has special meaning. Deepest appreciation to John and Barb Wojcik and Jack and Lynn Katilius. Without exceptional friends like these and like Jim and Jacque May of Cherokee, North Carolina, life would be very different.

Working with the PMI Publications Staff has been a real joy. Jim Pennypacker has developed a professional and customer-focused team. My deepest appreciation to Bobby Hensley, Sandy Jenkins, Danell Moses, Mark Parker, Shirley Parker, Michelle Triggs Owen, Ann Wright and all the others who worked to make this a "quality book" in more ways than one. A special thanks to Jeannette Cabanis, my editor, whose hard work, skill, and creativity—combined with her patience—helped make this book a much better product.

Chapter 1

Why is Total Quality Management Different on Projects?

Far and away the best prize that life offers is the chance to work hard at work worth doing.

Theodore Roosevelt

JUST BEFORE HE left work one crisp fall afternoon, John Picard received a phone call that was destined to keep him from sleeping that night—not because of worry, but because he was excited. The big award had been announced: John would be managing the largest project of his career.

The preliminary schedule for John's new project forecasted two years to completion, but John knew that the client wanted the project finished early. Even though the budget estimate of $250 million reflected good information, John's division had had some recent experience with budget overruns, so there would be pressure from management to keep his cost down.

Driving home that evening, John developed an organizational structure in his head and began developing his management plan. The management team proposed for this project had been hand-picked by John and represented the kind of experience and team approach needed on a large, complex project. The project included some technical challenges, the kind of challenges that would keep Geoffrey McCoy's technical staff interested. Geoff, who had worked with John on the project plan, had the knowledge to understand the technical needs of the project and the skills to manage the project's largest group. John had known things were going his way when Geoff agreed to join the project team as the technical manager.

Danny Baxter, he thought, had joined the project team because of his experience in international procurement, experience that the project would need to be successful. He knew that Danny had just finished a big project and was eager to get started again.

Andre Riviere was another key person on the project team. Andre was the most experienced controls manager in the company, so John knew he would get good cost and scheduling information from him.

John, who believed strongly in the value of the project controls manager, thought of a favorite saying: "Good information is the feedstock of good decisions."

As the plan came together in John's mind, one piece of information just didn't seem to fit. Lucy Mills, who would be the project administrator, had worked with this client before. When he'd stopped by her office to share the big news, she'd mentioned that this particular client would expect the project to be managed using total quality concepts. Although John had gone through the company's training courses on total quality, he wasn't at all sure that he could use this training in a project environment. Tomorrow, he thought, he'd get with Ken Troy. Ken was one of the company's total quality consultants, who were assigned to key projects. He had been assigned to John's project when the company understood the client's desire for a TQM approach to managing their project. Once he had a handle on the total quality requirements, John thought, he could finish the project management plan.[1]

With all the parts of the project coming together so swiftly, John knew this would be one of those years when he would enjoy getting up each morning and going to work. Still, as he and his wife Judy talked late that night about the project, they promised themselves to plan long weekends and vacations to make sure that John didn't get too wrapped up in his work.

"It's not just your time with me I'm concerned about," Judy said. "It's your health, too."

John knew she was right. He'd just turned fifty, and his trim body reflected his love of exercise. He was one of the few project managers in the company who ran daily, even when he was out of town. Running was one of John's key methods of reducing the effects of stress. His two daughters were grown, with families of their own, so he usually found it easy to make time for fitness in his day. Now, however, with this big project on his plate, he knew it would take thoughtful planning to keep his personal life from being overshadowed by the demands of work. But he promised Judy he would make it a priority.

THE NEXT MORNING, John asked Ken to spend an hour helping him develop a total quality approach to the project. Because they had worked together before, John knew Ken was bright and often added

---

[1]For a brief overview of project management and TQM concepts, see Appendices A and B.

useful insights into project issues. Ken was particularly helpful when relations sometimes got strained with a client; now John would be asking him to advise him on issues internal to the project itself.

John had watched his job as project manager evolve over the years. Projects were more complex and his role demanded a greater focus on people issues. More and more clients were made up of teams with different backgrounds. Concern for the environment, greater emphasis on safety, diversity in the workforce, were all changes that made sense but took time away from running your project. It seemed like every piece of correspondence was written by a lawyer and every project had some international component to it.

John knew that this project would mean a next step in developing his project management skills, but he was just as determined not to try and be anybody but himself. Ken might have good ideas and understand the client's expectations, but this would only work if two conditions were met. First, these ideas had to make sense to him. John would not implement a new approach that did not meet the common-sense test.

Second, and just as important, any new approach had to be consistent with John's basic approach to management. A focus on people and renewed attention to the client made sense and was consistent with John's management approach but the rest felt a little soft. John wanted to stay open-minded, though. If Ken had something to offer, he wanted to be the first to implement it into his project management approach.

KEN RESCHEDULED HIS morning so he could meet with John and arrived an hour before lunch.

"How do I include TQM in the management plan of the project?" John asked.

"What aspects of our approach do you think need to be emphasized?" responded Ken.

John's hesitation showed that he was unsure where to begin. He said, "Well, I was thinking we would discuss how we monitor our processes to meet specifications, but I'm beginning to think we need a broader approach. Get me up to speed on our company's approach to total quality."

Q, TQ, TQM

"Just a couple of years ago," Ken began, "we defined and focused on quality as meeting specifications, fitness for use or conformance to requirements. If we translate these concepts into project management terms, a quality project is a project that meets the standards established in the scope of work."

"What about total quality? Is there a difference?" asked John.

"Total quality seems to be a more recent concept, a vision of doing everything right the first time. The vision aspect captures the concept of the unachievable, something to work toward that drives our present activities," explained Ken.

Ken waited a minute while John thought over these remarks. He had worked with John before and knew that he often punctuated conversations with short periods of silent thought.

Finally, John asked, "You've talked about quality and total quality, but what about Total Quality Management?"

"Total Quality Management focuses on the customer. Meeting the customer's needs, providing value to the customer, meeting the customer's reasonable expectations, are all ways of expressing customer preeminence," said Ken.

"Meeting the customer's *reasonable* expectations." John frowned. "Who defines what's reasonable?"

"That's one of the reasons we found that definition lacking," Ken said. "Our company's definition of Total Quality Management is *the application of skills, tools, techniques, and processes to understand, manage, and meet customer expectations*. This definition has two characteristics that appeal to project managers like yourself. First, it's action-oriented—the application of skills, tools, techniques, and processes implies doing things, making something happen. The second aspect of our definition focuses on meeting customer expectations."

"Then a total quality project is one that applies skills, tools, techniques, and processes to understand, manage, and meet customer expectations?" asked John.

"Yes." Ken nodded.

John had recently attended a workshop on TQM, and when he participated in a workshop he usually developed a good grasp of the topic. What Ken was telling him sounded different from what he remembered. John had a reputation in the company for being cerebral, of thinking and talking like a college professor. He enjoyed writing for professional journals and thinking about those aspects of project management that made his profession challenging and exciting. Now he zeroed in on the characteristics of the company's definition that didn't match what he'd learned at the workshop.

"What about leadership, culture, values, innovation, and continuous performance improvement? I attended that two-week workshop on TQM just last month, and you haven't mentioned a single topic that we discussed, sometimes in great detail."

"I agree with the importance of concepts and approaches to total quality such as culture, leadership, and values, but we have learned a great deal about applying total quality *to projects,*" answered Ken. "The differences between applying TQM to projects and applying TQM to the manufacturing or continuous process environment reflect the differences between *project* management and *general* management.

"You have a master's degree in project management and belong to a professional organization that promotes the development of project management skills. You have refined, adjusted and developed new approaches and techniques to management that are more appropriate to projects. We've done the same thing with Total Quality Management on projects."

"Good management skills are necessary in both the manufacturing and project environment," countered John. "A good project manager builds on those skills to meet the difference in approach that the management of a project requires. Are you saying you developed an approach to Total Quality Management that builds on the approach used in the manufacturing environment?"

"Not exactly," Ken responded. "We looked at our definition of Total Quality Management and asked, *What skills, tools, techniques, and processes do we need to understand, manage and meet customer expectations on a project?*"

"Wouldn't those skills be the same?"

"Not necessarily, because projects offer some challenges that require different skills, tools, techniques and processes."

John knew it was time to start structuring his thoughts, so he went to the whiteboard on the wall and began to list some of the differences between a project environment and a manufacturing environment. First he wrote:

CUSTOMER

"In manufacturing, the output of every work process has a customer, and the total quality program focuses on understanding and meeting the customer's requirements. That would seem just as true on my project. All the work we do has a customer and our project's total quality program helps us define and meet customer requirements."

Ken agreed, adding, "Understanding the requirements of each work process is important for both projects and manufacturing. It's the foundation of the improvement process."

For the next few minutes John added several items under "Customer" on the whiteboard:

Understanding customer expectations

- identify the customer for your work process
- understand the requirements
- develop your work process so that it meets the customer's requirements every time
- improve your work process.

"Isn't this the process for meeting customer requirements?" asked John.

"The process you just outlined is a technique of Total Quality Management," answered Ken. "We look at work processes that, when added together, produce a final product. It's this final product that must meet the expectations of the ultimate customer and the ultimate customer is the one referred to in our definition of Total Quality Management.

"You see," he continued, "understanding the requirements of the customer is different between manufacturing and projects. In manufacturing, the customer who pays cash is the ultimate customer. All the work processes, when put together, produce a product that the ultimate customer buys. Understanding and meeting the ultimate customer's requirements is the focus of the total quality program. Because manufacturing has a thousand ultimate customers, companies do customer surveys, demographic analyses of customer's habits, and all the other things a marketing department does to understand the requirements of the company's customers.

"But our projects typically have only one customer. That customer may be a small team, but it is a team that reflects one need. The techniques and processes we use to understand the requirements of the project's customer are very different from those used by the marketing department of a manufacturing plant.

"One tool we used on the Miller Project was a monthly client survey," Ken continued. "This was a simple tool that asked the client to rate how well we were doing on seven key areas of the project. Each area was rated on a scale of one to ten with space for comments. I sent the survey to nine important members of the client team each month and the response rate was always high. It was an opportunity to give us critical feedback and the client took advantage of it.

"The survey helped in several ways. First, when the clients helped me to develop the form, they were also helping us identify what was important to them. The second way the survey helped was to provide constant feedback on performance. We used this information to focus on areas that were important to our client. Sometimes we had to go back to the client to get a better understanding of an issue, but usually we understood the concern and could address it in a timely manner. Occasionally, we needed the client's help in solving a problem and this process made it easier to get the help we needed."

Ken paused thoughtfully, then added, "The surveys helped us in another important way. They helped us manage the client's frustration level. We know that clients feel various levels of frustration during the life of a project, and how they deal with those frustrations impacts the team's performance. On the Miller Project, these frustrations were dealt with monthly in a positive way. We took the issues that came out in the survey very seriously and tried to solve every issue that came up. This kept issues from growing or getting out of hand, and the client always saw our efforts to address the issues."

Ken further explained how the survey prevented issues from piling up. By airing issues monthly, they could be dealt with proactively. "Even if a client has small issues, so small they're not included in the survey, the slate is wiped clean anyway because they have an opportunity to address them in the comments section. Without this opportunity, small issues continue to build, as they always do on a project, until a catalyst comes along and opens a dialog, which usually digresses into a catalog of misdemeanors committed by the project team, as you know."

"That is certainly true! I can agree that our approach to understanding the customer's needs has to be different," said John. "What would be a second difference in our approach to Total Quality Management?"

"How about time?" asked Ken.

"Okay." John wrote:

TIME

"I think I know where you're going with this one," he said. "If I make an improvement that saves me $100 per month and costs me $2,500, I break even in 25 months and from then on I make more money. On a larger scale, that's how we justify the cost of this project.

"But on a project that lasts only two years, a $100 per month improvement will lose money if it costs $2,500. The improvement process on a project must look very different from the improvement process used in a plant."

To his list John added:

Improvement Process

as a subheading under "Time." After standing thoughtfully in front of the board a minute, he then added:

Team Building

"What are your thoughts about team building?" asked Ken.

"A large part of the total quality training I received focused on how to work together to achieve common goals. We have a lot of customers who have implemented self-managed teams in their plants. They do a lot of training and have a lot of meetings before the teams start seeing improvement in performance. Dedicating six months to a year to developing a team is considered a good investment in a plant, but on most of our projects, the project would be over before the team came together. So developing a team approach on a project has to be significantly different from the approach we discussed in the total quality training."

"How else will the time constraints of your project affect your approach to TQM?" Ken prodded.

"I never thought about it this way, but projects are discrete, one-time, endeavors with a defined beginning and end. The manufacturing plant is a continuous process that will only change significantly when the outside environment forces change," admitted John. "So I need to think about a beginning and an end to the project. How will I get the project on the right track and keep it there?"

"Try asking that question another way," Ken suggested. *"How will I know what the right track is and how will the project team know when they are on the right track?"*

"So I have a couple more bullets to add to my list," John said." He wrote:

FOCUS

and

MEASUREMENT

As he wrote, John recalled a discussion he'd recently had with a friend who was the local hospital administrator. His friend had bragged that they had built a work culture in the hospital that was the envy of the industry. The hospital's five-year plan included developing a work culture that was customer-focused, promoted innovation, and encouraged a sense of pride in the work of the hospital teams. Because the hospital culture developed by the administrator and his staff was in place, a new employee entering the hospital could very quickly understand how she contributed to the goals of the hospital, her role and responsibilities, and how to measure her performance. The new employee would pick up cues all around her on what was expected.

John recalled this conversation now because he knew that he didn't *have* five years to develop a total quality culture. The hospital had a lot more time, but also had a barrier that John didn't have: they had to change an existing culture. John, on the other hand, was starting from scratch. He knew that even though he didn't have much time to instill a total quality culture, new ways of approaching work were much easier to implement on a project.

John turned to find Ken patiently waiting for him to re-engage in their conversation.

"Because we are managing a project, a discrete endeavor, the project team will need to develop a way to focus the project. We will not have the structure and organization of a plant. The project team can set up any type of organization we believe will be successful, knowing it will go away in two years," explained John. "But we must define very clearly what we want to achieve, who is responsible for the various parts, and track our progress toward our goals so we will know if we are making the right kind of progress."

"Looking at what you've written on the board, I see that defining what you want to achieve is *Focus* and tracking progress toward goals is *Measurement*," said Ken, "but where have you referred to defining who's responsible for the various parts of the project?"

John added to his list:

ROLES AND RESPONSIBILITIES.

Suddenly, glancing at his watch, John said, "I have a meeting with Jane Roberts in 15 minutes, and I'm still not sure I can explain how I'm going to approach TQM on this project. As executive sponsor of the project, she expects a complete management plan. What I need today is to demonstrate that I have a plan for implementing TQM on this project. What I have on the board just talks about what I need to do, not *how* I'm going to do it."

19

"One element you may want to emphasize is the need for the project team to buy into the plan," suggested Ken, "and the best way to get buy-in is for team members to help develop the plan."

"This issue is on the agenda for the project team meeting this afternoon. We can put together a plan on how we will implement TQM on the project at the meeting," thought John out loud. Then he thanked Ken for his help. "You've helped a great deal and I definitely want your comments on our plan," he said. "I'll get back with you in a few days."

John now knew what he was going to say to Ms. Roberts *and* what he was going to do in the project team meeting. Things were coming together. He copied his notes from the board before he started confidently toward Jane Roberts' office.

The man with a new idea is a crank until the idea succeeds.

Mark Twain

Project Management Plan: Use of Total Quality Management

Customer
- More narrowly focused definition of customer (as opposed to broad definition used in manufacturing)
- Understanding customer expectations; more personal because I can get closer to my client
- Identify the customer for your work process
- Understand the requirements
- Develop your work process so that it meets the customer's requirements every time
- Improve your work process.

Time
- Improvement process (shorter payback time on projects)
- Team building (creating a culture, not changing one)

Focus
- Need process to focus project quickly

Measurement
- Develop measurements that help keep the focus

Roles and Responsibilities
- Need process that will help people understand how they contribute to project success.

Met with Ken Troy today, preparing TQM plan for the project.

We defined TQM as the application of skills, tools and techniques to understand, manage and meet customer expectations. I like this way of defining things because I can get my teeth into it. TQM stuff has always seemed kind of fluffy and useless to me. Maybe we can do something on my project that demonstrates some kind of value.

This is more than just common sense management. Lucy is telling me I will need to hone my listening skills but she is implying that I will need to be more focused on leadership issues of the project and less on management. I always felt I was a good leader. That's how I got this far in the company. Now it seems the bar has been raised and expectations are higher or at least different. It will be hard NOT to hear the wrong message.

My first reaction to Ken was that I know what I am doing. I have been successfully managing projects for years. But when I listen closer like Lucy suggested, there is really a new focus. Maybe subtle, but I feel like Jane Roberts, the client, Lucy and Ken are saying "execute this project differently." I wonder if they trust me. I have good skills but I will have to be careful not to become defensive.

Leadership principle No. 1: "Attitude makes a difference." I am going to use this project to take my leadership skills to new heights and model the new age project manager. Now all I have to do is figure out what that means.

I still don't have a good feeling about all this, but I want the client team to know I am open to new ideas. At this point I am trusting Ken. I hope he knows what he's doing.

Chapter 2

Client-Focused, Goal-Directed and People-Oriented

I will name you the degrees [of argument]. The first, the Retort Courteous; the second, the Quip Modest; the third, the Reply Churlish; the fourth, the Reproof Valiant; the fifth, the Countercheck Quarrelsome ....
William Shakespeare in As You Like It

THE PROJECT TEAM meeting was scheduled for 2:00 p.m. As usual, Lucy Mills arrived early to arrange the room and get prepared. John had asked her to join the team as project administrator, to supervise project accounting, and to coordinate the administrative needs of the project. Lucy had worked with the client before, so she knew the importance of the Total Quality Management approach. She'd also worked with John before, so she knew she would have a chance to shine. John was the type of boss who shared the credit for success.

In the ten years she'd worked for the company, Lucy had worked hard to develop a good reputation and gain the recognition of her peers as a valuable member of any team. She knew she was good at what she did, and a large part of her self-esteem was linked to her professionalism. Lucy commanded respect without demanding it. She demonstrated competence with a style that built confidence in people.

Danny Baxter arrived just as Lucy finished setting up the room. Danny had transferred from Chicago for this project because his expertise in international purchasing was definitely needed. He folded his lanky basketball player frame into one of the chairs and gave Lucy his rather shy smile as a greeting. Danny's surfer-boy appearance belied a keen, focused personality. He'd developed a structured approach to negotiating that focused on details while creating a negotiating environment conducive to relationships that benefited both parties. Danny had been around the company for a while and knew that large, complex projects received a lot of management attention and the politics sometimes got brutal. He'd decided that the best course of action was to lay low, do your job, and stay out of the way.

Geoffrey McCoy saw Danny and Lucy talking in the meeting room, but since John wasn't there yet, he decided to squeeze in one more phone call before the meeting started. Geoff's technical expertise gave him credibility among his technical staff. He also had an organizational approach that was respected by everyone in the division. Geoff was known for asking the right questions, for separating out the important things from the streams of information that crossed his desk, and for a sharp wit that would occasionally cut you to pieces. Most people believed that Geoff was headed for a leadership position in the company. Although many considered him a demanding boss because of his ambition, John counted on him as an honest and straightforward member of the team. Geoff's technical staff would be the largest group on the project, so Geoff knew he would be a key figure.

Just as Geoff finished his phone call, Andre Riviere and John entered the meeting room, chatting about the horses Andre raised on his farm—Andre's favorite subject.

"As you know, John," Andre was saying in his distinctive French-Canadian accent, "I'll probably retire after this project, so I really want it to be something special. Then I'll be content to spend more time in the stables." Andre was thinking, *If the project is managed right, I can put in a good eight hours each day and then go home to Marie and the farm.* He believed in keeping a good balance between his life at work and at home.

Andre took a seat and pulled his trademark candy bar from his pocket. At over six feet tall and 220 pounds, he looked like an athlete, even though he never played sports.

"More health food, Andre?" cracked Geoff. "Ice cream, candy bars—I don't get it. How do you stay in shape?"

Andre answered only with an expressive shrug and a smile.

JOHN STARTED THE MEETING by reviewing the agreement with the client. With the next few items, they started putting the project plans together. Each team member expressed an opinion on what needed to be done before they met with the client. A plan began to come together. With about thirty minutes left before the office closed, John introduced the TQM issue.

Geoffrey McCoy immediately focused on the issue: "What deliverables are expected, when are they due, and how much extra effort is required to meet these deliverables?"

"It's not that easy, Geoff," responded Lucy. "The client expects us to manage this project using Total Quality Management principles. If we do it right, there won't be any additional deliverables, and it will take less time, not more."

Seeking clarification, Geoff asked, "What are the TQM principles?"

"There are three basic Total Quality Management principles that are important to our client," answered Lucy, as she wrote on the flip chart. "Our project must be:

Client-Focused
Goal-Directed
and
People-Oriented.

"*Client-focused* means aligning with the business goals of the client," Lucy continued as she turned back to the team. "It means developing goals around what's important to the client. It means we need to measure our client's perception of our progress toward meeting his goals, as well as measuring schedule and cost goals. It means we had better be able to hear his issues even when they are being whispered. It means our success directly and proportionally ties to our client's success."

Lucy stopped and looked at the team. Was she talking too much? She looked at John and he gave her a slight nod that said "keep going."

"*Goal-directed* means we truly understand what we need to accomplish to be successful," Lucy continued. "That everybody on the project understands how they contribute to the project's success. If you asked me today what three things we need to accomplish this month to be successful, I could give you an answer but it would probably be different from Danny's. Shortly after the kickoff meeting, if our client asks two people that question and gets different answers, we will get some strong feedback. We will spend a lot of time on the project developing, agreeing and tracking goals."

Lucy paused and took a deep breath. "*People-oriented* is more difficult," she began.

"If you tell me 'people are our most important asset,' I will choke," interrupted Geoff. "People just don't believe that bull anymore. Too many words and not enough action."

"I think you have hit on the key, Geoff," answered Lucy. "Our client expects action. We know how to motivate people, to develop effective teamwork. When we develop a list of those things that impact morale on a project, our list is great and reflects some of the best thinking in our industry. Our client expects us to translate these concepts into

25

action. To develop a focused approach that maximizes the contribution of everybody on the project. He also expects us to recognize and reward people as the project progresses. This is NOT a client who feels he hasn't got his money's worth unless he leaves a drained and exhausted team behind. He IS a client who realizes that, if a team enjoys the project, they are more likely to be successful and be in harmony with the type of culture that exists in the client's organization.

"One more important point here," Lucy added. "Our client is very proud of the empowering culture they have built and they will not tolerate a relationship with us that has a negative impact on that culture."

A couple of minutes of silence passed before Andre put in, "That's all well and good, but that's not going to help us plan this project." Since Andre was responsible for scheduling project activities, this discussion created a little discomfort for him. Most project activities were very similar from project to project. Now Lucy was saying the activities would be focused on goals that meet the customer's expectations. Although it sounded easy enough, the process seemed a little fuzzy, and Andre liked to work with hard data.

"The key," offered Lucy, "lies in understanding the client's expectations, defining the activities that meet those expectations, and developing measurements to track our progress against those expectations."

"I've worked on over twenty projects, and the client has always wanted the same thing," Danny interjected. "Bring the project in under budget, ahead of schedule, and meet all the specifications."

Lucy had had this discussion before. At the beginning of most projects, people were usually skeptical. But she knew the quality culture would begin to take hold over time and that people would begin taking ownership as optimism replaced skepticism. Lucy also knew the project needed Danny and Geoff to lead the process because they would play such an integral role on the management team. She began to relax a little when Geoff started responding to Danny's comments.

"Danny, your clients may *say* that's what they want," said Geoff, "but do you remember the Walkingstick Project? We came in three months late, two million over budget, and the client *loved* us. They thought we were miracle workers. We're still doing projects for them."

"We *were* miracle workers on that project. We saved the client ten million dollars over what it *should* have cost him," responded Danny, with an expression of pride.

"Yeah, but remember the Pulliam Project?" asked Geoff, hitting his point even harder. "We met every specification on the project, saved over a million dollars and completed the project on schedule. The project didn't have a single hiccup." Geoff paused for effect, then continued. "The client was so angry that he still refuses to return our phone calls. I doubt we'll ever get work from them again."

"They gave us the wrong specifications!" declared Danny. "We had no idea how that project fit into their long-range plans; they should have told us. What were we supposed to do, guess?"

"That's my point: it's not always cost, schedule, and specs," said Geoff. "There are other things that matter to our clients and we'd better learn what those expectations are."

John stepped in, as he sometimes did to get the group refocused. "Lucy," he said, "in general, what can we learn from your last job with this client?"

"First, you'll be surprised at the client's openness. If we don't know what the client wants on this project, it will be because we aren't listening," responded Lucy. "On the other side of the coin, they expect us to be just as open, sharing our concerns about the project, including them in problem solving, letting them know how they can contribute to solutions, and keeping them truly informed about the progress of the job.

"Let me share with you a model the client sometimes uses to explain what they expect to receive from the total quality efforts."

Lucy went to the whiteboard and drew a box divided into four parts:

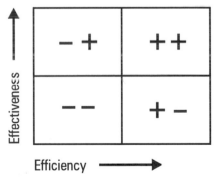

"The client refers to a two-dimensional model, where the vertical axis represents 'effectiveness.' How effectively do we do our work? Effectiveness refers to our earlier discussion on customer satisfaction,"

"Last month we told them to rotate
the stock in the warehouse.
But the orders they got said 'rotate the
warehouse'. Yep, this is gonna cost us."

explained Lucy. "The measure of the project's effectiveness is directly related to the degree of customer satisfaction with the project. Effective activities are those that focus on meeting customer requirements.

"The horizontal axis on the client's model represents 'efficiency.' How efficiently do we do our work? How efficiently do we use our resources to meet customer expectations?

"By using this two-dimensional model, we have developed four categories of activities. Category one, the lower right box, includes activities that are done efficiently, but not effectively. For example," said Lucy, "if we called maintenance to repair the door next to the water fountain and a guy came and fixed the door in the next room, he may have fixed the door meeting all specifications, under budget, and on time, but he did not satisfy the customer because we wanted the door in *this* room fixed. As silly as this may seem, we all know there are activities on all projects that fit this category."

"I can give you several examples from our last project," said Andre drily.

"Andre," Geoff interrupted, "let Lucy finish the model first. I want to hear this all the way through before we start telling war stories."

"Come off it, Geoff, I was just trying to support Lucy," Andre responded.

"No offense meant, Andre, but we are not going to have time for a lot war stories on this project. We've got to stay focused."

"I didn't plan to tell WAR STORIES," Andre said, a little louder.

John held up his hand and gave a small shake of his head. These small gestures usually got people's attention. He made a quick judgment that people were tired. He knew both Andre and Geoff would probably talk about this little interchange later. Anything he said now would just make things worse, so he just nodded to Lucy, who took up where she had left off.

"The second category, the upper left box, represents activities that were done effectively, but consumed more resources than were needed," Lucy continued. "If the maintenance chief had then become angry and sent a crew of ten people to fix every door on the floor, she would expend a lot more resources than were needed to fix our little project, the door by the water fountain. That was effective, but not efficient.

"Then there is the case, the lower left box, where maintenance sent ten people, and they *still* didn't meet the customer's expectations. We wanted the door fixed so that it wouldn't hit the water fountain, but they fixed the squeak in the door," said Lucy.

"The fourth category, the upper right box," she added, "represents activities that are both focused on the client and are completed with minimal use of resources. These activities bring maximum value to our clients. In our case, a carpenter came and fixed the right door, the right way, the first time.

"The goal of Total Quality Management is to move activities into the fourth category, thereby increasing effectiveness and efficiency. Every project has activities in all four categories. The processes and tools of Total Quality Management do not usually eliminate all ineffectiveness or all inefficiency, but they do increase our ability to help our clients be competitive."

"Sorry, Lucy, but I just don't get it," said Danny impatiently. "We aren't fixing a door. We're executing a multimillion dollar project. Just showing a model of becoming more efficient and effective doesn't help us do that."

"I think I'm beginning to see where Lucy is going," said John, as he contemplated Danny's comment. "We have to be both effective and efficient. We have to do the right things and do things right. Ken has talked about client surveys, a two-day workshop with the client, and a goal development process that focuses the project activities on what's important. These techniques can help us be effective. Workflow diagrams, quality teams, and certain measurements help us do things right—that is, be more efficient—in our work. I think Lucy is right. We will never be 100 percent effective or 100 percent efficient, but our success depends on how well we use these techniques to improve our effectiveness and efficiency."

The team sat for a while thinking about what John just said. Finally Geoff turned to Lucy. "You've painted a great picture, Lucy, of how to make a customer happy. But do we really have the resources and time to take on any additional tasks?"

To keep the team focused, John answered for her. "My understanding is that if we do this right, we will *save* on time and resources, am I right, Lucy?"

She nodded.

"So what's the next step?" asked Andre, glancing at his watch.

"Ken has mentioned a two-day workshop with the client to get a handle on client expectations," said John. "I'll get with Ken and see if we can get the ball rolling on that. If there's no other business we need to discuss today, I'll see you tomorrow."

The meeting had run fifteen minutes late. John knew people were thinking about heading home and hoping that this late initial meeting didn't mean that this project would be like so many others: evenings and Saturdays, meeting deadlines, fixing problems. *Well*, he thought, *it's like the president of the company always says—if it was easy, he wouldn't need us.*

Change means movement. Movement means friction. Only in the frictionless vacuum of a nonexistent abstract world can movement or change occur without that abrasive friction of conflict.
                                        Saul Alinsky, in "The Purpose"

30

John's Journal

The staff meeting went a little rough today, talking about concepts and philosophies. We need to get down to the action plan or I will lose the team. These are action-oriented people who have a need to develop goals and plans for achieving goals.

The team seemed a little tense, but no more than usual for the beginning of a project. Geoff is taking a lead role, as I thought he would, but he still has to develop working relationships with the other members of the management team. After the meeting Geoff walked with Andre back to his office. Although Geoff comes across hard at times, he is able to build bridges with people. His drive will be important to the project success but his ability to create trust in his relationships will be a bigger contribution to Geoff's success.

Geoff asked about Ken's role today. A continuing discussion. I'm beginning to feel more comfortable with Ken around. Although nobody seems to know what a quality facilitator really does, he listens well and gives team members valuable feedback. Even during the proposal stage, I noticed that this team is developing a little faster than I've seen before.

Ken doesn't attend all our meetings, but the meetings he does attend have a different atmosphere, even when he doesn't say anything. It is like driving down the road and seeing a policeman. You may not drive differently but you focus more on driving carefully and within the law. It's the same with Ken.

I think more about the team development and the impact I am having on developing a good team when Ken is in the room. I think everybody is a little more focused on team dynamics and we spend a little more time on the process as well as the content of the meeting. I don't know if this is it but our meetings are more effective and becoming more pleasant.

Geoff suggested that Ken was the only one on the team who was only interested in the success of the project. Then he corrected himself by adding that, of course, that assessment did not include me! But he's right. Every member of the management team has a department to run and the success of their department is extremely important to them. I have seen some project managers use this pride to maximize the contributions of the individual parts of the project. This never seems to work because you lose the synergy of the project management team. Although this is hard to quantify, this team focus on project goals, not department goals, is key to success.

Because Ken doesn't have a department his observations are not made to position his department or negotiate any interdepartmental issues. His feedback is honest and only represents the focus of the project. Because he is not the boss and his feedback seems to have a unbiased validity, his contribution helps us remain focused on project goals, not functional or personal goals.

Chapter 3

Preparing for the Focusing Workshop

Transport of the mails, transport of the human voice, transport of flickering pictures—in this century as in others our highest accomplishments still have the single aim of bringing men together.
                    Antoine de Saint-Exupéry in Wind, Sand, and Stars

KEN AND JOHN met for breakfast the next morning. Ken, in his continual losing battle against weight gain, ordered the mixed fruit bowl, while John relished his eggs, bacon and a side order of pancakes.

"So, you were going to tell me what I need to do to prepare for this two-day workshop?" asked John, as the conversation turned to work.

"Your preparation is minimal, John," said Ken. "But your leadership in getting the client and our key people enthused about the workshop is important. Our workshop location should be of some help, too."

"It was easy convincing Jane Roberts that we needed to find a 'getaway' for our workshop," remarked John. "It's good working for a boss who understands that getting out of the office is a valuable way to free up the brain for some creative thinking. Having the workshop at a retreat in the Smoky Mountains also sends a message about the importance of this workshop to management. If we are spending this kind of money, we must be serious."

John remembered the previous spring, when he and Jane Roberts had met with several company managers to revise the marketing plan. They had used the same retreat, and John could still smell the aromas of the wet forest surrounding the lodge, and of the fresh-baked bread from the kitchen. The retreat's atmosphere had had a dramatic effect on that group of uptight executives. The milieu contributed to a creative work session, one that developed a plan with consensus support. John was glad this workshop would be held at the same retreat. He wondered if they would get the same kind of outcome.

Visioning

Where there is no vision, the people perish.

The Bible, Proverbs 29:18

He asked Ken, "What else can I do to get ready?"

"Instead of thinking about what you need to do to start up the project in the next couple of weeks, think about how the project will look when we're finished," answered Ken. "In other words, develop your vision for the project. Don't put it into words, but try to understand what must be accomplished for the project to be a success. This will become your vision of success."

"I remember reading somewhere that the most successful Olympic athletes visualize themselves crossing the finish line in record time or throwing the javelin an incredible distance," John mused. "The process of *visualizing* success actually helps an athlete's performance."

"It's the same principle. Visioning also provides two key benefits for our project," Ken went on. "A project vision statement provides a common definition of success. That means we can check any activity on the project by asking, *Does the activity help us achieve our vision?* And, it provides a method of communicating where the project is going. It's like a beacon in the storm. When the project waters get rough, which we know they will, the vision statement is there to give guidance."

"I can understand how developing a vision statement with the client would take some time, but how are we going to use up two whole days?" worried John.

"Let's go back to the definition of Total Quality Management for a minute," said Ken. Remember our definition is *the application of skills, tools, techniques, and processes to understand, manage, and meet customer expectations*. The workshop is one of the processes we use to understand, manage, and develop a plan to meet customer expectations.

"The workshop begins with some team building activities. This is the first time the project management team will get together. Although most of the team members have met each other, these activities will give the group a chance to begin developing a team identity, to provide a structured learning experience for looking at some project issues and to start breaking down some of the natural barriers that exist when people come together for the first time.

33

"The group will then develop a 'Project Charter.' The project charter defines why we are doing the project. In a way, it puts boundaries around the project. This is our understanding of what our client, and our company, has chartered us to accomplish," Ken continued. "A charter is very similar to a company's mission statement. As if we were on a journey, the charter tells us where we are going, while the vision statement tells us what it's going to be like when we get there."

"How do you write a charter statement, or for that matter, write *anything* in a group setting?" John shook his head skeptically. "One of the things that teams do poorly is writing."

"I'll divide the workshop into three teams," Ken explained. "Each team will use a brainstorming process to develop a list of key elements that must be included in the statement. Then they'll discuss the list, reach consensus on the most important elements, and assign a representative of the group to develop a statement from the list. Each of the group representatives will then present that group's statement to the entire team, including the flavor of the discussions, and answer questions. Finally, I'll take all three statements and, with selected help, write a single charter statement. I usually do this during lunch or in the evening break and bring it back to the entire team later for fine-tuning and final acceptance."

They both ate in silence for a moment. Ken had been helping projects focus on client expectations for the past two years, so he knew John was thinking, *How long will this take, and how much will it cost?* John, like most project managers, was action-oriented. In John's view, spending time defining the purpose of the project and understanding client expectations might be necessary, but let's get it done as quickly and effortlessly as possible. Ken knew that John's commitment to this new process would only come after he realized success, but Ken needed John's enthusiasm *now* to set the right tone for the project.

"This process of developing a charter and using the same process to develop a vision statement takes some time, usually a couple of hours for each statement," Ken went on, answering John's unspoken questions. "But, both the process and the products bring benefit to the project. During these small group discussions we listen to Hal, the client, talk about his expectations for the project, about what *he* has been chartered to do by his own organization, and his vision of what he wants to accomplish. We can hear if there are discrepancies between different people on the client's team. Are they together or do they have different—and more importantly, conflicting—expectations for us?"

34

"We also have a chance to express our own expectations," added John. "How do we perceive our charter? What's our vision of success? How well are we melded into one team? I can see how that would be of value. But how does this process relate to our total quality program?"

"Remember that part of our Total Quality Management definition is *'to understand, manage, and meet customer expectations,'*" said Ken. "During the two-day workshop, our task is to listen very carefully to the client's expectations. If these expectations seem unreasonable, this is the time to discuss them. Most project clients have a good understanding of how the project fits into their overall strategic plan and an understanding of the cost of the project. If our client has underestimated the costs or overestimated the project's likely performance or contribution, we must bring our expertise to the table to help bring these expectations in line with reasonable projections."

John took issue with that. "Most of our clients are pressing for higher performance and lower cost by the project team. We can't just tell them, 'Our experts say you are being unreasonable.'"

"Of course you're right, John," responded Ken. "But this process does help manage these expectations in two ways. First, a person may have been thinking about what he wants and expects for a long time, but until he *expresses* these expectations they usually remain just a mental note— which may evolve as the project progresses. But by having to express his expectations clearly now, the client may modify them to meet the more structured environment of a presentation. If our client has developed some real wild expectations over time, he has to think about them now and ask himself if they are really reasonable."

"Are you saying that for most people, just asking the question, 'Is this reasonable?' can change the way they think about an issue?" asked John.

"Yes, and it's a question that's often not asked," responded Ken. "We too often discover what could easily be called unreasonable expectations only after we fail to meet them. Even though we can sometimes change these expectations, we still leave the client with a feeling that we cannot meet his expectations."

"I see what you mean," John thought out loud. "Most of the time, people make decisions based on their feelings about an issue. If the client feels that his expectations were not met, then his evaluation of the project, and maybe his contribution to its success, will suffer."

"Right. By discussing expectations and what it takes to meet those expectations, we develop a mutual understanding of what it takes to accomplish our work," said Ken. "This helps the project in a second way. By listing these expectations, we can develop a plan to meet them and help define the client's roles in meeting his own expectations. People do not always understand the role they play in determining project success. By defining what the client wants, determining what it takes to get there, and the role the client plays in making this plan work, we can track everybody's contribution to project success, including the client's."

The restaurant began to clear out as the breakfast crowd headed to work, but John still wanted a better understanding of what would take place at this focusing workshop.

"Okay, now we have a charter and a vision statement, what are we going to do with them?" he asked.

Goal-setting

"We are going to identify the three to five goals we must accomplish as a team to achieve our vision," answered Ken. "These are not lofty goals that would be nice, but the results that the project *must* achieve in order to be a success."

"I could list twenty goals right now that the project must accomplish," said John.

"One of the key purposes of the focusing workshop is to provide project focus. We will take everybody's twenty or thirty goals for the project and narrow them down until we develop consensus around three to five of the most critical. Other goals, activities, and milestones on the project must in some way support these goals," explained Ken.

"Why only five?" asked John. "We may miss a critical goal if we are too narrow."

"Because the more goals we have the greater the likelihood that we'll lose project focus. There's no magic number, but a good rule of thumb is to pick a number that everybody on the project can remember. If you ask a technical person assigned to this project, 'What are the key goals?' how many can we reasonably expect him or her to easily remember? My experience suggests that the number is between three and five."

"If you have goals," said John, "then developing a plan to reach those goals seems like the next logical step."

"That's right. We'll take each goal and identify barriers and potential barriers to accomplishing the goal," said Ken. "Then we'll develop action plans that effectively deal with the barriers *and* efficiently achieve the goals."

"That seems like a lot to accomplish in two days, "said John. "If you have even five goals and spend an hour identifying barriers for each goal, you've eaten up five hours without even starting on action plans."

"Four hours are allocated during our two-day workshop to develop action plans," said Ken, "and that should be enough to get us started at this stage of the project. First, we will divide into teams with each team taking one or two goals. Small teams can be more efficient than larger groups in detailed discussions and brainstorming. Second, the goal is not to finish the process but to get the process started and develop a plan for completing the process."

The waitress filled their coffee cups again, prompting John to check his watch to see if he really had time for more coffee. Ken knew he had to summarize the rest of the workshop quickly so that John could get back to the office. John seemed to be comfortable with the direction of the meeting plans, so Ken thought he probably would not want much more detail.

"Once we have goals and have started on action plans, we'll develop a method to track our progress," continued Ken. "These are project assessment tools. They tell us how well the project is doing toward meeting our goals and achieving our vision. Most of our projects have good tools for tracking cost and schedule but are less effective in tracking goals that are not cost- or schedule-related."

John thought a minute and then said, "If we can identify the client's *key issues* and mutually define *measurements* that track the project's progress against those issues, then we can build the client's confidence in our plan and in our tracking against that plan. That way, even if we get behind, the client will be more comfortable because he knows exactly where we are and can be part of our recovery plan."

Ken agreed. "After developing goals and measurements for those goals, we can then discuss *roles and responsibilities*," he said, trying to move the conversation along. "Then we can focus on our role and the client's role in making the project a success. Sometimes these lists can get lengthy, depending on the detail the team needs to be comfortable with their own roles as well as the roles and responsibilities of other key players. This is the time to clear up any misunderstandings and develop a document that identifies the key players' roles and responsibilities."

"Can you include a discussion on the roles and responsibilities of the joint management team?" asked John. "I'm not sure everybody understands how we are going to operate as a team. Maybe we can draft an agenda of a typical management team meeting."

37

"That's an excellent idea, John. I'll put it on the agenda right after the individual roles and responsibilities.

"You know, we need to hurry if you're going to make your nine o'clock appointment," said Ken. "So let me add just a couple of short points. Throughout the workshop, we need to emphasize that the workshop is just a beginning, that the efforts to keep the project focused must continue throughout the life of the project. The workshop will be hard work, but there's no reason people can't have fun at the same time. We will do what we can to make the environment and process enjoyable while meeting the workshop objectives."

"Developing a vision, generating goals and action plans, and defining roles and responsibilities—an ambitious two days!" said John.

"Can you think of a better way to spend two days?" Ken joked.

I agreed to think about my vision of project success and I'm trying to honor that promise. It's not easy, but I find I am seeing this project a little differently. Because I am looking so far out I am developing a different perspective of the project and of what we need to do to be successful. Focusing seems like a good word for what we will be doing. I am beginning to look forward to the Focusing Workshop. I'm still not sure what some of the items on the agenda will do for the project, but I am going to support the process and put some trust in Ken. Based on my discussions with Ken, I think it will go something like this:

Workshop Agenda

Vision Statement

Team Building

Project Charter

Goals

Barriers/Potential Barriers

Action Plans

Progress Measurements (tracking progress)

Roles and Responsibilities
⇒ individual
⇒ joint

HAVE FUN!

Chapter 4

Interlocking Teams

... man is a free creative spirit. This produces the very queer world we live in, a world in continuous creation and therefore continuous change and insecurity. A perpetually new and lively world ... A world in ever-lasting conflict between the new idea and the old allegiances, new arts and new inventions against the old establishment.

Joyce Cary in Writers at Work

ABOUT A WEEK after the focusing workshop, Danny, Andre and Geoff met for their weekly lunch together. These weekly lunches, begun the same week the project was announced as an unofficial opportunity, gave them a chance to compare notes and talk about ... whatever. Despite their status as the project's key functional managers, the group declared at their first lunch that their first priority would be to have an enjoyable break together and *then* discuss the project if something needed discussing. Nevertheless, every week the project became topic number one—and today was no exception.

"Although it was a lot of work, I enjoyed the workshop," Andre began the conversation. "I always enjoy the Smoky Mountains and the food was great."

"I have mixed feelings about having that kind of meeting at a mountain retreat," responded Geoff. "We clearly had a relaxed, creative environment and the way the meeting was conducted indicated that both our company and the client's are committed to this process, but I wonder if the technically oriented people of my department understood the value of this type of meeting?"

"I know that, for me, this is the first time that I really believe I understand the expectations of the client," Danny said. "I have a clear understanding of who's responsible for what and how my team will be measured on this project. I've always known the role procurement plays on projects, but now I can develop a plan with my team that focuses on the unique needs of this project."

"It was a good meeting," admitted Geoff, "but I've been through this kind of thing before. Everybody is singing on the same sheet of music now, but wait until a serious problem pops up and you'll see all that work go down the drain. The positive effect of the workshop will deteriorate over time."

Danny disagreed. "A lot of what happens later on the project depends on us. I've seen the process work and believe the benefits depend on how well we develop our plans, provide feedback to our teams on progress of the plans, and work together as an integration team."

"*Integration team.* I don't know if I can adjust to that," said Andre. "We've used *project management team* so long, I don't think the terminology will change on this project even though we agreed to the new terminology at the workshop. I know we want to communicate the need for decisions to be made at the lowest level, and our most important function as a management team is to integrate the various functions within the project—but we are all *managers*, and managers are trained to make decisions."

"Everybody on the project will be making decisions," answered Danny. "Even though as managers we are responsible for making key decisions, our primary task is to communicate to the members of our teams the project's mission, vision, key goals, and measurements and the role our teams play in the success of the project. We communicate the project's progress and each team's progress in supporting the project. We also coordinate with other teams on and off the project, and the best place to do that is in the integration team meeting. Integration team is a good term and it communicates the function of the team better than management team."

"That's sounds great," said Geoff skeptically, "but we didn't even finish our action plans at the workshop. We started projects with this kind of enthusiasm lots of times in the Buckhannon office, but we lost momentum very quickly. Trust me, the integration team will start making more and more decisions. By next month we'll be the project management team again. Every manager I've ever known started out the project with a "Theory Y" approach to management, you know— empower your people—but by the end of the project they were all "Theory X" managers."[2]

---

[2]See Appendix C for an explanation of Theory X-Y management styles.

"If we do this project like the last one," answered Danny, "the work we did at the workshop will spread throughout the entire project. It depends on the functional teams and us as team leaders to maintain the momentum."

"That's easily said, but I have the largest team on the project," Geoff pointed out, "and the schedule pressure requires us to use every available hour making progress. How am I going to make schedule deadlines and do this extra work for the integration team?"

"Your participation in the integration team is *part* of your job, one of the most important parts. The way we function, how we communicate, and the tone we set in dealing with each other will set the tone for the entire project," Danny responded. "I have seen projects where people are so busy doing their jobs, they don't have time to attend meetings, complete reports or even read or respond to e-mails. These projects always end up with problems and, quite frankly, these are problems the *team* should have predicted and prevented. But these problems begin taking more and more time of the team members and eventually the project team begins receiving help from upper management. When the project starts getting help from upper management, plan on twelve to sixteen hours a day for the duration of the project.

"Sorry," Danny said a little more softly. "I've been there and it's not pleasant. I've thought about this a lot and I agree with John and Ken, the team approach is key to functioning smoothly and maintaining some kind of even keel during the life of a project. And this project is organized around teams!"

Danny pulled a pen out of his shirt pocket and began to illustrate his words on a paper napkin. "Look. Every person on this project is a member of at least one team. The project vision, goals, and measurements were developed by the project integration team and will be communicated through the functional teams. I'm responsible for the procurement function and, therefore, the leader of the procurement functional team. It's the interlocking team concept. In procurement, we develop a functional team vision, goals, and measurements that support the overall project. Our teams are then empowered to develop action plans that meet these project objectives."

"Each team will have team members who will be members of other teams, on which they have significant interface and must work together to achieve success for that team and the project. That way all the teams are interlocked in such a manner that they share information and, when necessary, resources, in the most effective way for the project."

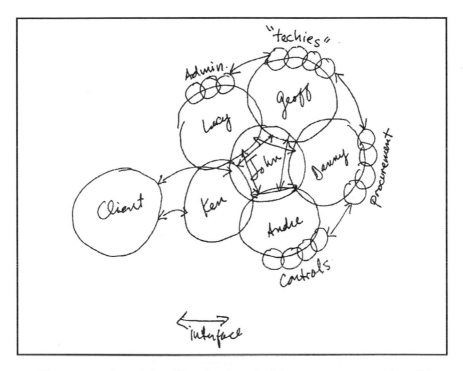

Danny continued detailing the interlocking team concept, describing how the goals of the integrating team would be supported through all the other teams on the project by linking membership. Every team would have at least one member who was vertically connected to, as a member of, the integration team. And every team would have at least one member who was horizontally connected to, as a member of, the other functions on the project that would have significant interface with this project. Goal setting, anchored in the project's key goals, would spread throughout the project, and communication on these same issues would flow back to the integration team.

"Actually," Danny frowned at his sketch, "you can't really show this is two dimensions; the interrelationships are too complex. This makes it look like my function isn't integrated with Ken and the client—which isn't true. You'll just have to imagine it."

Danny lectured with the enthusiasm of a recent convert. He passionately expounded the power of the interlocking team concept in focusing the whole project on the key project goals and supporting communication throughout the project. But when Danny looked at Geoff, he realized Geoff had stopped listening five minutes ago, so he stopped and waited for the inevitable rebuttal.

"But when the project peaks I'll have over 500 people on my team alone; I can't have team meetings with 500 people!" Geoff protested.

"Your team represents the technical branch of the project. You have leads for each technical department, and you will meet with them on a regular basis. Because every member of your team is a department lead, your team meeting is more like the project's integration team. The team members will then be responsible for their own team, which must develop goals and measurements for their portion of their work," said Danny. "That's how the interlocking team concept works. Every team is interlocked with the other teams of the project through joint team membership at key interfaces."

"That means if I have a team for each major technical branch, I'll have at least ten major teams and maybe as many as fifty subteams altogether. If you spend two days developing a team vision, goals and measurements, that's two times fifty or 100 days of people in workshops. I can't afford that kind of time," retorted Geoff.

"You won't need that kind of time because the more technically focused the team, and the more homogeneous, the less time it will take to develop a plan, because homogeneous team members have similar backgrounds, education, and vocabulary. These similarities make it easier to arrive at consensus," Danny offered as he finished his hamburger. "The functional teams will also take less time because they have less work to do. They'll be building on the work of the integration team, not starting from scratch."

"Wait a minute," Geoff said. "What's this about homogeneous teams? The team we put together came from the same pool of people we always use, and this client's people look very much like most of those of the clients we normally do business with."

"Think about who's on the team." Danny counted them off: "Andre from controls, John from project management, Lucy from administration, me from procurement. The client has representatives from the business unit, operations, maintenance, and computer systems. Even though all these people will work on the project, they all have different backgrounds and educations, and they'll look at the project from different perspectives. Sometimes during the workshop we had difficulty agreeing on issues simply because we didn't understand what the other person was talking about.

"Remember when Tom was talking about the tax implications of certain approaches to the project? I was lost during most of the conversation. It's not because I'm dumb—it's because he deals with these issues every day. If I dealt with them every day, I'd understand

GLASBERGEN

"At lunch I devised this brilliant team organizational chart on a napkin. Unfortunately, you're not on the team anymore because I had to wipe some gravy off my mouth."

his issue without the long discussion. One time I had to ask a question three different ways before he understood what I was asking. That's *not* a homogeneous group."

"Everybody on my team went to different schools," said Geoff. "Don't you think that will make it more difficult?"

"No, because even though they went to different schools, they were trained in the same discipline, and people trained in the same discipline are even more likely to think alike than people who went to the same school. I don't know if people who think a certain way naturally choose the same career or the career develops a certain way of thinking, but I do know that people who do the same kind of work tend to think alike."

"So how will that shorten the time?" pressed Geoff.

"A homogeneous team shares the same terminology or language; they have comparable experiences, and they have a similar understanding of how to work together," answered Danny. "Once a functional team has an understanding of how success is defined on this project, they can develop very quickly a definition of how their team contributes to that success. The majority of the functional team's time will be spent identifying both real and potential barriers to that success and developing action plans to surmount these barriers."

"Then why did the workshop we went to last week take two days?"

"Mainly because the participants were from different companies, different functions, and different disciplines. They needed time to understand what each person was saying and why that was important. Then we needed to meld those issues into a common understanding and commitment to project success.

"Remember, we're not talking about different processes," added Danny. "All the teams will be interlocked through a common process of defining the team's vision of success, developing key goals, and an action plan for achieving these goals. What's different is the makeup of the team, which will allow the functional teams to go through these processes much more efficiently."

"I've got twenty minutes before my one o'clock meeting," said Andre. "Let's get some ice cream before we go back to work." The group headed for the ice cream dispenser, where the conversation quickly changed to a casual debate on the best movie playing that weekend.

Andre thought how different this was from his last project. People could disagree, argue their thoughts strongly, and still remain good friends. It was a good feeling. Andre knew this was the way to run a project.

He that wrestles with us strengthens our nerves, and sharpens our skill. Our antagonist is our helper. This amicable conflict with difficulty helps us to an intimate acquaintance with our object, and compels us to consider it in all its relations. It will not suffer us to be superficial.
Edmund Burke in Reflections on the Revolution in France

I've asked Ken to spend more time with Geoff and his team. Ken seems to help us look at the big picture a little more. Geoff may be approaching this with a formula, trying to write policies and develop a budget to cover TQM. His team members were getting a little on edge because they saw new expectations without understanding how they would be judged. They were applying old rules and trying to manage the project with procedures. The first meeting with Geoff and Ken must have been very uncomfortable for everybody because we were talking about concepts people knew about but didn't know how they applied to our everyday work.

I know that Danny, Andre, and Geoff are struggling to implement the interlocking team concept. How many teams, how much time is invested in team meetings, and how do we share resources are just a few of the questions I hear. Even though there's still some confusion, I see fewer barriers between teams. These guys are breaking down traditional walls between functions and creating an exciting team spirit. Although we may not have it down right yet, we are using the interlocking team concept to integrate the project both vertically and horizontally.

Chapter 5

Managing Client Expectations

*I know not anything more pleasant, or more instructive, than to com-
pare experience with expectation, or to register from time to time the difference between idea and reality. It is by this kind of observation that we
grow daily less liable to be disappointed.*
       Samuel Johnson in Boswell's Life of Samuel Johnson

E ARLY ONE EVENING, as the last few cars left the office parking
lot for home and families, Ken sat in John's office discussing the
integration team meeting. The meeting had gone well. Although
the project was still in an early phase, everything was happening on
schedule. But something was bothering John.

"Do you think the client is pleased with our approach to the
project?" asked John.

"He's been a part of developing the approach with us," said Ken. "If
he wasn't happy with our approach, I would think we'd know it by
now."

"Clients aren't always that open about what they think. You know
about my last project. We did a good job. One of the best projects I've
managed, but the client was not happy in the end. He admitted that
we'd met all the criteria in the project scope but said the project should
have gone better. I don't know why it ended so poorly because we
started out great and maintained a good relationship until the last
stages of the project. It wasn't the project's performance—the client's
expectations were a moving target, and that caused the project to look
poor. I don't want that to happen again."

"A client always feels frustration during the life of a project," said
Ken. "How well we manage that frustration probably determines how
the client views the success at the end of the project. We may want to
develop a plan to manage that frustration."

"Speaking from experience, clients aren't always open about what
they're feeling. How do we know when the client is frustrated?" said
John.

"There are usually symptoms," responded Ken. "When the client is late for meetings, doesn't attend meetings, is slow to return phone calls, these are all signs of discontent. When a client feels uncomfortable with the team, he won't tell you that. He'll give you a credible excuse like pressures from the boss, but ...."

They exchanged a silent, knowing expression. Then Ken and John spent the next hour planning how the project team could better understand the client's expectations, measure how well the project was meeting those expectations and increase the client's comfort level with the project. Together, they outlined for the project team a:

Plan to Meet Client Expectations

1. Educate the client from the beginning on what it takes to get the job done

"After years of experience executing projects," Ken said, "the project team understands the phases and frustrations of projects. Because of this experience, periods of frustration are taken in stride. The team understands the events that lead to the frustrations and knows how to deal with them.

"These same experiences can be much more disconcerting for clients. By explaining what to expect and planning with the client a process for minimizing the impact of these concerns, the team prepares the client for these events and reduces his frustrations."

2. Clarify expectations

"There are three important points under this heading," said Ken.
- Ask specifically what the client expects and develop a written statement of expectations. This goes beyond the scope of services and addresses how we deal with each other and work together.
- Develop measurements for meeting the key expectations. Using these measurements, provide feedback on performance to the project staff throughout the life of the project.
- Don't let the expectations or measurements change arbitrarily.

3. Establish standards and procedures for decisions

"Making decisions is one of the project team's most important tasks," Ken noted. "Make sure every team member understands how and when to bring up issues, concerns, and problems. Also:
- Develop procedures that encourage both the client and the project team to bring issues and concerns to the table early.
- Develop a process for dealing with each of these issues and concerns effectively. Define how and when decisions are made.

49

"He's a great customer, but he's very thrifty. He wants us to e-mail five tons of freight to Cleveland."

- Use weekly staff meetings, action item lists, decision lists, responsibility matrices, and other tools to clarify issues and foster decision-making on a timely basis."

4. Deal early with the tough issues

"We often believe we can solve problems, improve performance, or make up for mistakes in such a way that our client doesn't become aware of the full implications of events that might have a negative impact on the project," Ken said. "But the greater the distance between the time of the event and the time the client knows about the event, the greater the client's frustration and mistrust.

"Including the client in problem analysis and recovery planning provides him with confidence that problems are being addressed, that he can positively impact problems on the project, and that the team is not hiding problems from him."

5. Provide mechanisms for revisiting key decisions/issues

Ken elaborated, "The project environment often moves fast, with decisions made and implemented to keep pace. But once a decision is made, is the project committed forever to that decision? The obvious answer is 'No.' But how does the project team address issues or decisions that have been settled? It may take significantly longer to make decisions if they're viewed as final—and a slow decision-making process can have a significant impact on the project schedule."

6. Manage the project around milestones

John remarked, "During the life of a project, a small problem often creates a small delay. Enough small problems delay the end date or slip the schedule to the degree that the project team has to work overtime, make rushed decisions, and add resources to finish the project by the end date. This frantic atmosphere isn't the impression you want the client to remember, but since it's their last impression, it's usually a strong one."

"To combat that tendency," Ken responded, "create a small number of milestones that reflect significant progress toward completing the project. Manage each of these milestones as if it represented the end of the project. Add resources, work overtime, and make all reasonable attempts to meet these project milestones. This spreads the pressure over the life of the project instead of building toward a frenzied finale."

7. Celebrate milestones with your client

"This I can't stress enough," Ken stated. "Build on your success. Celebrate your progress and include the client in your celebration. This helps the client understand his contribution to that success and provides a balance for the tense times on the project."

8. Include the client on teams, give him responsibility, and make him a part of the solution

"On too many projects, the client acts merely as overseer, making sure all the rules are followed. But project success depends on the active involvement and contributions of the client," Ken explained. "One way to achieve this involvement is through the client's participation on the team, not just as another person who attends team meetings, but as an active contributor who develops solutions to problems and actively helps implement those solutions. Because project problems are client problems, project success becomes the client's success."

9. Clarify values

"Understanding the values that are important to the client … communicating your own values … resolving discrepancies between value sets ahead of time. This is the most significant contribution you can make to improving communication on the project," Ken said. "Disagreements based on differences in values are extremely difficult to mediate, because compromise means compromising your values—and

51

that kind of compromise comes at a high price. Understanding differing values and planning up front how to deal with conflict significantly reduces the potential for insoluble conflicts on the project."

10. Deal evenly with the client

"The client must know he can trust the information he receives, trust that decisions are made with his best interest in mind, and personally trust the members of the project team," Ken said.

"I couldn't agree more," John nodded. "Opportunities to take advantage of the client always present themselves, but although these may realize a short term benefit, a breach of trust, more than any other single act, gives the client a negative view of the project."

BY THE TIME THEY WENT HOME that evening, John had more fully developed his list of ten principles for dealing with the client. He planned to pull the staff together for an informal work session so they could discuss and improve on these principles. He knew that it would be tough to engage the staff in this type of discussion, but by the time the meeting was over, the team members would know how they contributed to the client's expectations of project success.

Nothing sets a person up more than having something turn out just the way it's supposed to be, like falling into a Swiss snowdrift and seeing a big dog come up with a little cask of brandy round its neck.
Claud Cockburn in Printing House Square.

John's notes:

Dealing with the Client

1. Educate the client from the beginning.
2. Clarify expectations.
3. Establish standards and procedures for decisions.
4. Deal early with the tough issues.
5. Provide mechanisms for revisiting key decisions.
6. Manage around milestones.
7. Celebrate milestones with the client.
8. Include the client on teams.
9. Clarify values.
10. Deal evenly with the client.

I'm developing an understanding of what it means to be "Client-Focused." It's NOT a buzzword—but it's also not an easy concept to explain. There are no activities, no work processes ... being client-focused is more like an attitude that is reflected in everything I do on the project. I believe I'm getting better at putting myself in the client's shoes, understanding what the project means to the client's success beyond the project, and how we can help him get there.

The plan we developed for managing client expectations this week is only common sense. It's the way I want to deal with Hal and his team all the time. It means including Hal in the planning of the project and being painfully honest with him when we run into problems.

My job is to make Hal, as well as all clients, a Hero—someone who was wildly successful at managing the project.

Chapter 6

Maintaining Balance

Think in the morning. Act in the noon. Eat in the evening. Sleep in the night.

William Blake in The Marriage of Heaven and Hell

ON SATURDAY MORNING, John walked up the steps to his office. He was going to miss his regular Saturday workout to write some long-overdue letters, so taking the stairs made him feel a little better. He'd tried to write letters at home but just couldn't keep his focus. Maybe if he immersed himself in an environment where he was used to concentrating on tasks, he could spend four to six hours and mail the letters on the way home. If he could get done in four hours, he would still have time to run five miles before going home. After writing a month's worth of letters, he thought, he would need the stress relief that exercise provided.

As he neared his office, John noticed Geoffrey McCoy's door open. Although John had expected to be alone in the office, he wasn't really surprised to find Geoff there. Geoff was good at his job, and he put in a lot of hours—maybe too many.

John hesitated for a minute; he really did want to write the letters by noon, but thought maybe he should talk to Geoff. He put the stationery on his desk and headed for Geoff's office.

"Hi, Geoff," he said as he knocked on the door jamb. "No golf today, with the weather so great?"

"I wanted to get these effort-hour projections completed. It looks like we're under budget by about ten percent, but I need to run these projections to make sure."

John quoted Oscar Wilde's contribution to the project manager's sanity: "Life is too important to be taken seriously."

"Don't give me your *what-are-you-doing-here-on-Saturday* look," Geoff said sternly. "This project would not be the success it is if it wasn't for me and a lot of other people giving those extra hours. Besides, *you're* here, too."

"Geoff, I appreciate the job you've done on this project. You're a key part of that success you just talked about. You've pulled together a great team and have kept it well-oiled. But you put me in mind of a lunch I had with Dr. Andrews when I was doing my graduate work in project management."

Geoff thought, *That's just like John.* He would subtly point out an area where improvement was needed, give you some specific praise and then tell you a story or give you an example. *Good thing he's such a good storyteller*, Geoff thought, suppressing a smile, *or this job would be unbearable.*

AS A GRAD STUDENT, John had been determined to graduate with a perfect grade point average. He had attended classes full time while his wife Judy earned the family income. Although he didn't realize it, John harbored a lot of guilt about not being the family provider, and this drove him to prove himself with high grades.

Although Dr. Andrews, the project management department head, didn't know why, he knew John was driving himself mercilessly. Dr. Andrews was one of those professors who took a personal interest in his students, and he saw John driving himself beyond reasonable expectations for any student. When he talked with John's other teachers, he learned that John read everything he was assigned— something no student ever did. He invited him for a lunch at Maggie's, where you could buy a good meal on a student's income.

During lunch, Dr. Andrews had encouraged John to back off a little, not to worry so much about grades, and to focus on the things that he wanted to learn and which would help him in his career. Probably the most important change that he recommended was effective time management. That lesson had helped more than anything else in John's long career as a project manager.

Every night John had been staying up late to complete his reading, studying each day's notes. He didn't go to bed until he believed he had done everything he was supposed to do that day. Sometimes that meant operating on four or five hours' sleep. Often Judy wouldn't see John except when he ate. Dr. Andrews seemed to know what John was doing and made one succinct suggestion: *Go to bed at a reasonable hour each night and get a good night's sleep. If you can't get everything done, only do what's important.*

John reluctantly took his professor's advice. Every night at eleven o'clock he would go downstairs, where he and Judy would watch *M*A*S*H* on the bedroom television.

"Dad, when you're done with your report would you like to log on to an interactive laptop kid?"

After a couple of days he began to get the drift of prioritizing work and his performance started improving, while his study hours decreased. Since he only had a limited number of hours, he had to use those hours effectively. That was the lesson he tried to convey to Geoff on that November Saturday.

"And you know," John concluded, "I still can't hear the opening music to *M*A*S*H* without remembering those precious hours watching TV with Judy."

I am convinced that a light supper, a good night's sleep, and a fine morning, have sometimes made a hero of the same man, who, by an indigestion, a restless night, and rainy morning, would have proved a coward.

Lord Chesterfield *in*
The Letters of the Earl of Chesterfield to His Son

John's Journal

I spent some time with Geoff at the office today. He's sharp as a tack but he had better listen to my "grandfatherly advice." He needs to remember what's important, both at home and at work, and focus on those things that are important. Although I'm glad we had a chance to talk today, he should have been out playing with Geoff Jr.

Chapter 7

Using Teams on Projects

Persons grouped around a fire or candle for warmth or light are less able to pursue independent thoughts, or even tasks, than people supplied with electric light. In the same way, the social and educational patterns latent in automation are those of self-employment and artistic autonomy.

Marshall McLuhan *in* Understanding Media

MONDAY, ON HIS way to see Ken, John puzzled over something Hal Campbell, the client project manager, had said during their weekly "let's talk about how things are going" meeting. Hal had read an article in a total quality journal discussing the use of self-directed work teams in a nearby plant. Now he wanted self-directed work teams on the project. With the project management team, functional teams, ad hoc problem-solving teams, and duration-reduction teams, how could the project benefit from yet another type of team?

John knew that many of the departments in the client's plant were now introducing team concepts as part of their total quality program, but projects already had a strong history of using teams. Because projects often use matrixed organizations, which are temporary, developing teams had long been recognized as an efficient way of doing business. So using teams was not new to John, but he had only a vague idea about self-directed work teams. That's why he headed for Ken's office.

Ken was on the phone but waved John into his office, raising one finger to indicate that he would be done in a minute. After Ken hung up, John said, "Hal Campbell wants us to use self-directed work teams."

"What do you want to do?" Ken asked.

"I don't know," said John. "I'm not sure how we can use self-directed work teams. I'm not even sure I know what they are. That's why I'm here."

Ken spent some time bringing John up-to-date on self-directed work teams and how the client was using them in his plant.

"Most, if not all, of the total quality literature proposes the use of teams as a method of improving quality within an organization. The use of teams as a tool for implementing total quality makes sense because the appropriate use of teams increases communication, increases customer focus, provides a method of empowering and motivating people, and provides a systematic process for addressing common barriers. The appropriate use of teams results in an increase in the product or service quality, an increase in creativity and synergy, lower costs, and reduced cycle time. With these benefits, it's easy to understand why organizations are searching for ways to implement the use of teams in every aspect of their business.

"When Hal looks at implementing total quality on the project," Ken continued, "it's a natural inclination to recommend self-directed work teams because this approach has demonstrated so much benefit to the continuous process parts of the plant's organization. Yet, the history of teams on projects, along with some unique aspects of projects, seem to indicate that an uncritical application of the self-directed team approach may be less successful on projects."

"Wait a minute," John interrupted. "Start at the beginning. What's unique about self-directed work teams? I've got to go back to Hal and either describe how we are going to implement self-directed work teams or explain why we're not."

Self-Directed Work Teams

"Self-directed work teams are teams that function without the traditional management structure. They conduct most, if not all, the traditional managerial functions *as a team*, without someone designated to make those decisions. Through consensus, they make decisions about work processes like scheduling work, determining work hours, and vacation time. Some teams talk with customers and suppliers about how to improve the entire work process. Sometimes, teams even make hiring and firing decisions. Most importantly, they are charged with improving their work processes. So most organizations that use self-directed work teams are flatter organizations with a highly motivated workforce that is constantly improving. When it works well, these companies are highly competitive."

"What do you mean, 'when it works well'?"

60

"It's a difficult and time-consuming task to develop self-directed teams," answered Ken. "Not all organizations have been successful in making the necessary changes in their approach to doing work that would allow the successful application of the self-directed work team concept. We are talking about a significant change in culture for most organizations. When someone has been successfully giving or taking orders for ten years, it is not an easy transition to start making decisions as a part of a team."

Ken knew John would not accept a short discussion. John liked to understand any new concept thoroughly, and Ken could see that spark of interest growing. John would not stop until he understood the concept, the strengths and weaknesses of the approach, and had explored how the concept might be applied to his project. He was exceptional in that way—always looking for new applications of ideas. That made his projects a joy for people who liked to be on the cutting edge of innovations.

Ken could tell the use of self-directed work teams had a strong appeal to John. But he also knew the questions that were running through John's mind: Was this an investment that would pay dividends to the project? Would it bring added value to the client? He could see that John wanted to know more, so Ken continued giving him more background.

"If It Ain't Broke, Improve It"

"'The use of teams on projects has a significantly different history than the use of teams within continuous process organizations," explained Ken. "The use of teams as an approach to total quality within the continuous process organization is relatively new. Prior to the quality revolution, specialization and standardization were the keys to increased productivity. Mass production mandated specialization and simplification, where parts and people became interchangeable and replaceable. One of the strongest elements of the total quality revolution was a change in thinking from 'leave your brain at the gate' to 'be creative and innovative in improving your work.'

"Teams are one of the most useful tools management has for tapping into the creative energies of employees," he continued. "The first attempts involved the use of concepts like quality circles, which focus on solving problems. Later, quality improvement teams focused on improving work processes rather than merely trouble-shooting, which promoted the saying 'if it ain't broke, improve it.' Self-directed work teams provided an additional element of empowerment and shareholding by team members.

"In contrast to team development within the manufacturing environment, the process of establishing a management approach for a project includes selecting the management team. People who may not have worked together before begin by defining the task at hand, the project scope, and developing a project structure that will accomplish that task. Since the project is by definition a one-time event, the structure is designed to meet the needs of that project, usually by the people who will run the project. Pulling together a team, a common and necessary occurrence in projects, is an event that takes extra effort within a bureaucracy."

John didn't respond right away. He just got up and stood thoughtfully, looking out the window. Ken sat in silence for what seemed a long time. Ken knew John would do one of two things: he would go away and ponder their conversation in depth, or he would immediately start asking probing questions. To Ken's surprise, John did neither; he just turned and said, "Okay, tell me more."

Ken gave him an example. "In the manufacturing environment, procurement policies and processes have been developed over a long period and have stood the test of time. They serve the needs of the organization well with little or no adjustment. On a project, the procurement person initially spends time with others, either individually or in groups, to understand their requirements and the requirements of the project. Even though a procurement standard probably exists, how it applies to a particular project needs further definition. A project procurement person must work with others to define the roles and responsibilities of their job and then refine procedures to meet the needs of the project."

"So what you are saying," said John, "is that forming a team is a natural part of developing the procurement and other structures of a project, but the procurement department of the plant has functioned successfully for years without teams and that the use of teams in the procurement department may actually upset the apple cart. It would seem that since projects have historically been more conducive to teams, there would be a strong correlation between the use of teams on projects and the use of teams in a manufacturing environment. But, if I'm hearing you correctly, you're saying that this isn't the case—that teams are developed differently and serve a different purpose within the plant environment."

Ken thought for a minute. John was on the right track, but he was going too far. A lot had been learned in the past few years from the use of teams in the continuous process environment of the plant, but not all those learnings could be applied without adaptation to a project. Ken didn't want John to reject everything, just to look carefully at the pros and cons of the more time-consuming aspects of some team approaches.

He tried to clarify it for John. "I mean that projects have a definite beginning and ending point and therefore a defined time for existence, and this reality impacts the use of teams in two ways. First, lengthy, time-consuming processes used by teams may not be appropriate for projects. Second, team processes involving relationships that evolve over a long period, such as self-directed work teams, may not have the time to become effective on a project.

"Teams that address improvement in a typical manufacturing environment are working within a system that has been successful. The team spends a significant amount of time analyzing work processes to develop incremental improvements. The philosophy of the continuous performance improvement effort can be summed up with the slogan, 'one percent improvement a 100 times versus a big win of 100 percent improvement.' The Japanese call this concept *Kaizen*. These improvements can provide a competitive edge in the marketplace and are a significant part of the total quality movement within the manufacturing environment, but the process is very time consuming. To define, analyze, measure, etc., can take weeks and even months before the work process improvements are integrated into the system. Projects just do not have this kind of time. Small improvements, so important for the manufacturing environment, may have little impact on the achievement of project goals.

"The use of self-directed work teams within the manufacturing environment has provided a breakthrough in empowering employees to improve their work processes. Self-directed work teams go through predictable phases in development. One description of a team's development phases is: forming, storming, norming and then performing.[3] No matter how this development is labeled or managed, self-directed work teams go through development phases that are less productive in the beginning. It may take several months before a significant improvement in productivity can be demonstrated. Typically it takes two years for self-directed work teams to demonstrate improved performance. Most projects would be completed before a self-directed work team could contribute to the project goals."

---

[3] For an explanation of these stages of team development, see Appendix D.

"My new approach to effective team development will take a bit longer. In my plan, we raise them from birth."

Ken looked at John, who responded by raising his eyebrows. John wanted the whole story and Ken knew he had to give it to him. If John was going to discuss this with Hal, Ken knew he wanted to be prepared.

"The use of teams has been a significant, if not essential, element of implementing total quality in the manufacturing environment," continued Ken. "However, some of the most successful uses of teams are not appropriate for projects. Most projects would be completed before most self-directed work teams reached the performing stage of development. Quality improvement teams that focus on the one percent improvements on very standardized work processes would typically have very little impact on the goals of the project."

John paced over to the window again. After a brief silence he turned and said, "You make a good case against the use of certain kinds of teams on projects. But we have used teams extensively on our project to develop project goals, develop our approach and identify potential barriers. In fact it seems that we're almost overrun with teams. How can we defend our successful use of some teams when you argue so effectively against a more advanced use of teams?"

"Oh, don't get me wrong. Teams used appropriately can contribute significantly to total quality in the project environment," answered Ken. "Functional teams, cross-functional teams, and task teams are three types of teams that can be used effectively to help achieve project goals.

"*Functional teams* are primarily characterized by membership from within a given function of the project," he went on. "For example, we have the project management team, Danny's procurement team, Andre's project controls team, and Geoff's technical team; these are all functional teams led by a member of the project management team. The charter or purpose of the team is usually twofold. Their primary function is to understand the project goals and establish functional goals and plans that support the project goals. Functional teams also analyze their work process to maximize performance and analyze interfaces with the function's customers, measuring the team performance through the eyes of these customers.

"*Cross-functional teams* are the second most commonly used teams on our projects. They promote the coordination between functions. Cross-functional teams focus on work processes that involve two or more functions. These teams flowchart the work processes, define the roles and responsibilities, and make sure that one function doesn't duplicate the work of another function. Their main role is to facilitate the smooth functioning of all parts of the project, but they are also chartered to drive improvements, looking for new or better ways to achieve project goals."

Ken stopped himself. "But we've had this conversation about teams on the project before. I'm covering ground that you can cover just as well as I can," he suggested.

"No, keep going, please," said John. "This helps me think through what I need to cover with Hal."

"Okay. The third team we use on the project is the *task team*," continued Ken. "Task teams are assigned a specific task to accomplish and usually have a relatively short time to accomplish their task. Early in our project, the management team set up two task teams. When it looked like the computer station was not going to work on our project, a task team was assigned to evaluate several alternatives and recommend the best course of action for the project. Geoff's technical people were the most represented, but the team included people from Danny's procurement and Andre's controls because they had information that was needed to make the best recommendation and would be effected by any decision. The team was given two weeks to make their recommendation, and they came back with a solution that kept the project on track. Again, for the project environment, this kind of team is a natural way of doing business, but for a continuous work process environment that has had a history of making recommendations and decisions through a hierarchy, this is a new and sometimes confusing approach."

John stood and put out his hand. Ken shook John's hand with a sense of accomplishment at having given John all the information he needed. At the door, John paused and glanced back at him. "Thanks again, Ken," he said. "You always seem ready with the right words. You do good work, and Hal appreciates it as much as I do."

Ken was amazed how much words like those continued to mean to him. John gave honest and frequent feedback and was almost always positive, finding a bright spot in almost every situation. His leadership and his style was contagious, and the atmosphere on the project was goal-directed and people-oriented. Ken knew how important that was because his last project had been just the opposite. Even though the project made money and was considered a success, many mornings Ken had hated to go to work. He'd actually put in fewer hours but felt more drained at the end of the day because of the strain in the workplace. He was glad to be working for someone like John.

There should be a sympathy with freedom, a desire to give it scope, founded not upon visionary ideas, but upon the long experience of many generations ... that in freedom you lay the firmest foundations both of loyalty and order.

W. E. Gladstone

John's Journal

Just when you think you have this TQM stuff figured out, something like this self-directed teams pops up.

I'm becoming convinced that I have it a lot easier than my counterparts in the manufacturing environment. Self-directed work teams make sense but I'll gladly let them worry about those "stormy phases" or whatever!

Project management may be behind in some parts of TQM but I know we have a lot to offer in the use of teams and empowering people. These have been good project management practices for years.

Chapter 8

All Teams Are Not Alike

ON A SUNNY, brisk November day, Danny Baxter and Geoffrey McCoy strolled back to work from the pool hall, talking. They still had plenty of time before Danny's procurement team meeting at two o'clock. The technical team had finished their meeting early, so Geoff had asked Danny to join him for lunch. A game of pool and the world's best hot dogs made for a terrific lunch break, especially when you had enough time to enjoy it. Today was one of those rare days.

As they walked, Danny and Geoff discussed the differences in their two teams. Geoff had a very structured group. Mainly technical people, they saw all meetings as a waste of time—yet they were the first to complain when information wasn't distributed efficiently. At meetings, they wanted a report on their measurements, a report on the project schedule, a review of the action items, and very little else.

Danny's procurement team was very different, and his team meetings were much looser. During meetings, the team looked at the project schedule, reviewed action items, and reviewed measurements, but spent a good deal more time discussing the various difficulties they were having with vendors. The procurement team members talked to vendors most of the day, discussed the project's requirements with Geoff's technical people, and always had to balance product specifications. They often felt like they worked "between a rock and a hard place;" if the specifications were too tight, they would drive the price up and when they were too loose, the product would not meet the project requirements.

As Danny and Geoff talked, they came to agree that each team had developed a style that matched the personalities of the group members. The types of meetings they were having were the types they needed.

Danny asked Geoff, "Have you ever heard Ken's stump speech on teams?"

"No," Geoff made a wry face. "Is this one of those stories with a heavy dose of symbolism?"

"Yes, with an equally heavy dose of sports," Danny laughed. "Ken will need to develop a new set of examples if he ever has a project with people who don't like football."

"Okay. Give me the shortened version."

"Ken describes three types of teams," Danny began. "Football, basketball and Olympic teams."

"Football and basketball I understand, but an Olympic team? This is starting to sound like one of Ken's better analogies!" Geoff was intrigued in spite of himself.

Danny described Ken's analogy of comparing the characteristics of work teams with those of sports teams, interlacing some of his own experiences with Ken's concepts. He began by defining a team as two or more people working together to achieve a common goal. With this definition, a team had three interrelated variables: the number of people on the team, how well the team works together, and how strongly they identify with the common goal.

"Let's start with the football team. The coach of a winning football team develops a strategy based on the opponent's tendencies and strengths compared to his team's strengths and weaknesses. He puts together the best talent he can based on that strategy and then drills the team members over and over again on how to execute their assigned roles. To be successful, each player must execute his assignment according to play. One person calls the plays and all the team members execute their assignments."

"I know that approach," said Geoff. "I was on a project in Tennessee where the project manager called everybody together and said, 'This is my team. You do what I say, and you can stay a part of it. If you can't be a team player, you can leave my team today.' I never thought of that project manager as a team leader, but by your definition, he may have been. He put together a good team, told us exactly what he wanted done, and we did exactly what he told us, and no more. Although I was glad to get off the project, the project was successful. We met all the schedule and cost goals and actually out-performed all the other project teams around."

"Then why did you want to leave that team?" asked Danny.

"Because it wasn't any fun!" Geoff exclaimed, than paused thoughtfully. "No, fun isn't the right word. The project wasn't a challenge. You did what you were told to do and went home. The only thing that mattered was doing your work on time and without mistakes. I like this kind of project better, where we're challenged to come up with new ways of doing things, where we're given a goal and we have to work together to achieve it. We're challenged to develop a

"Sports analogies are a powerful way to inspire teamwork. But next time use football, basketball or baseball—not duck-duck-goose."

plan that will achieve or exceed these goals. That means we must not only do our work, but coordinate effectively with others so we can work more efficiently. We aren't told what to do, we're expected to understand the goals of the project and work together to achieve them."

"You just described Ken's basketball team," said Danny, nodding in satisfaction.

They stopped by the lake outside the office and watched the ducks as Danny described the characteristics of a basketball team. "The winning basketball team has good players, just like the winning football team, but they execute their work much differently.

"When a play is called, each player understands what the team has to do to score, who's primarily responsible for shooting, and his own role in making the play work. The main difference with basketball is that each player has the freedom to freelance, to take advantage of new opportunities. They must watch how all the players react to the situation on the floor and adjust their play accordingly. Communication between players becomes critical. Much of their practice time is spent learning the tendencies and strengths of the other team members."

"Yeah, I would rather be on a basketball-type team than a football-type team, but don't let my old football coach hear that," Geoff remarked as he skipped a stone across the lake. "This is interesting lunch conversation, Danny, but let's get down to my favorite question: *So what?*"

"I knew that was coming!" Danny laughed. "Well, matching the right team style with the right project is the fun part." He went on to explain how projects are better served by developing a team approach that matches the needs of each individual project.

"The football-team approach is best suited for low-tech projects. Projects where the technology already exists, where outcomes are well defined, and where the company has good experience, are the perfect type project for this approach. The success of the project depends simply on executing the work efficiently. Team players have well-understood roles. Too much innovation can actually disrupt the project and reduce efficiency. There's little need to take chances.

"The basketball-team approach is best for high-tech projects, where the technology may be newer, where the outcomes are less well defined, and where the company experience is low or nonexistent. These are projects where you may need to discover a new way to make it work; they benefit from the basketball approach to managing the project team."

"But most projects are neither purely high-tech nor low-tech. They're usually somewhere in between," said Geoff. "What do I call that project that is halfway in between, a baseball-team project?"

"I hadn't thought about that possibility," said Danny. "But I'll give you Ken's spin on it. If we look at the project's technological challenge, how well the outcomes have been defined, and how much experience we have with this type of project, we can develop a good understanding of the type of team approach that would best meet the management needs of the project. If we need an innovative and moderate risk-taking approach, we know we need to call the plays, but still let the players freelance and take advantage of openings. If they blow a lay-up, it's all right, because they'll still keep driving the ball toward the basket. On a low-tech (football) project, players just need to understand their responsibilities and carry them out as expected.

"Basketball and football are the two extremes," continued Danny. "As a project moves toward the middle, you have to change your approach to match the needs of the project. You take the characteristics of the team that best match the conditions of the project."

As they turned to go back in the office building, Geoff grinned at Danny. "Are you going to make me ask?"

Danny smiled and shook his head. "The Olympic team approach would be a consulting type of project team. If you remember, Ken used to work with a consulting firm, where each team member worked for different individual clients. According to Ken, this was the loosest of teams. They had a common goal of providing top quality consultation for all clients, but work was graded and rewarded according to independent performance.

"Like in the Olympics," Danny went on, "each athlete must win his own race and that gold medal adds to the team's total—but it belongs to the athlete. The reward comes from your individual performance and no matter how poorly the rest of the team performs, your gold medal represents success.

"As a consultant, Ken could get advice and support from the rest of the team, but his success depended on his performance alone. Attempts by the leadership to build teamwork and team rewards were nice but wasted energy," concluded Danny.

They stopped at the door of the conference room where the procurement team was about to meet. "So, are you going to try to win a gold medal?" asked Geoff.

"Only if it's with the Olympic basketball team," laughed Danny, as he went into his meeting, leaving Geoff to think over Ken's analogy.

Geoffrey McCoy, Note to File: 0023A.17

File Under: Future Projects, Team Organization

When starting a future project, the following should be considered when setting up the project team.

FOOTBALL TEAM
    Project Description
        Low technology challenge
        Good company experience in executing this type of project
        High predictability in process and people
    Project Approach
        Tightly controlled
        Strong vertical communication
        Primary reinforcement, milestone achievement

2. BASKETBALL TEAM
    Project Description
        High technology challenge
        Low company experience
            Low predictability in process and people
    Project Approach
        Loosely controlled, empower people, team responsibility
        Strong horizontal communication
        Primary reinforcement, innovation

OLYMPIC TEAM
    Project Description
        Low coordination needed
        Individual initiative key to success
    Project Approach
        Individual goals and rewards

Chapter 9

"Look for Solutions, Not Blame"

How wonderful to have someone to blame! You may be miserable, but you feel forever in the right.

Erica Jong in How to Save Your Own Life

LUCY DRANK ANOTHER cup of coffee. She knew it was a mistake; coffee made her a little too tense for going home to the kids. But it had been one of those days and she just wanted a good hot cuppa java. She was about to call it a day when Chris Lester knocked on her door.

These late afternoon "stop bys" were not uncommon. Lucy had a reputation for being an easy person to talk to when you needed to work through something. Someone from the team had actually put a can on her desk with a sign saying "Psychologist—5 cents per hour" like Lucy in the *Peanuts* cartoon.

Chris had transferred from Tulsa, Oklahoma, the week before to start a major project for the company, and he was just putting his project team together.

"Lucy, have you got a minute?" asked Chris. "I've heard a lot of conversation about your project, and I'm a little curious about what you're doing."

"Come on in, Chris," answered Lucy. "What are you interested in?"

"I've talked with several people on the project, and I've picked up an enthusiasm and pride I don't think I've ever seen. I walked the project floor and saw signs like 'Innovation Street' and 'Value Avenue' marking where aisles came together, like street signs. When I ask someone about the project, I'd better have time to listen because I'm going to get a long commentary about its virtues. What are you doing differently?"

"We've applied Total Quality Management to our project," answered Lucy. "We've taken the time to set the project up the right way, and we have focused on doing things we knew were important but seem to somehow get lost in the chaos of starting a project."

"But how? What did you do different?" repeated Chris. Although his projects were successful and made money, he had never seen a project get the positive press that Lucy's project was getting. He knew he could get the straight scoop from Lucy. Was this real, and if it was, what could he take to his project?

Chris suddenly realized that Lucy had been talking for five minutes, but he had not been listening. He wondered about that, because he was usually a very attentive listener. Maybe the problem was that he just wasn't connecting with what Lucy was saying.

He broke in, "Lucy, I've got my first staff meeting tomorrow. What should I be addressing with the team?"

"Probably project principles," she answered. "Start by establishing a strong understanding of the values that are important for the success of the project."

"Come on, Lucy, I've got a scope with holes I can drive a truck through. The client thinks we can finish the job three months ahead of our present schedule, I believe the budget is too thin, and you want me to talk about *principles*? Maybe, if I had a client like Hal, that kind of meeting might make sense, but I need to bring some clarity to the project first."

"Chris, you asked," Lucy said softly. "Clarity comes from establishing a baseline from which we can plan out work. During the focusing meeting, we set a baseline by mutually developing a project charter and vision, defining roles and responsibilities, and developing a plan to achieve our vision.

"If you use one of John's boating analogies," she went on, "defining your scope and developing your budget and schedule are all ways of setting project buoys. They set markers for the planning of the project. You guide your project, like John sails his boat, using these buoys as markers to make sure you're going the direction you want to go. When you ask what markers are the most basic to project success, setting project values and principles begins to make sense. They set your foundation for setting goals, plans, and building your teams."

Chris thought about this for a minute. It was a little hard to buy, but he hesitated to discount what Lucy had said. He had learned from working with Lucy that she seldom presented something without thinking it through, and he couldn't think of a time when she was found to be off base.

"Give me some examples," Chris prodded.

"See the sign over my desk, the 'No Bats Allowed' symbol?" asked Lucy. "That's become an unofficial project logo. It represents a simple principle of the project: 'Look for solutions, NOT blame.'

"You see, for years, managers in this company have given people assignments and then, when people got behind in their work, they got out their baseball bats and starting clubbing them until their performance improved. Of course, the baseball bat is a figurative symbol for an attitude that prevailed and probably still prevails in this company. Some managers love using their baseball bats. We declared the baseball bat an outdated tool and outlawed it on our project. So that logo represents a basic value of this project."

"Lucy, you can't tell me you didn't have people problems on your project," scoffed Chris. "You can't run a major project like this without a myriad of people issues, conflict, performance issues, and stress."

"We've had our share of problems on this project, but we also had a basic value set from which we dealt with everyone," explained Lucy. "With the baseball-bat mentality, members of the team tend to hide things to protect themselves from abuse. People try to 'fix' things before management finds out. On this project, we wanted to identify problems early, so we could address the issues before they became big problems. Team members were encouraged to bring problems forward and were asked to help find solutions. When we addressed these issues the question was always 'What's the solution?' not 'Whose fault is it?' Occasionally, problems seemed so unbelievable that someone on the management team wanted to find the culprit, but John always reminded the team that we were looking for solutions, NOT blame. After a while you find various team members reminding the team to look for solutions. We then knew it was ingrained into our value system for the project."

"Okay, that makes sense. But how do you deal with just plain poor performance?" asked Chris.

"We approach people who are not meeting their goals with what we call 'the attitude,'" responded Lucy. "Members of the team are assumed to have the skills and motivation necessary to achieve their goals, so if goals are not being met, it must be because project management isn't providing something they need. We tell people this and ask them to help us understand what we need to do to help them accomplish their goals. Most team members respond when they see project management trying to help them meet their goals, rather than trying to catch them making mistakes. We aren't always successful, but we're more successful than we have ever been before."

"If you take away your manager's usual methods for motivating people, how do you develop and maintain motivation?" puzzled Chris.

"We believe that people *want* to do a good job and are self-motivated toward that end," answered Lucy. "They just want feedback on how well they are doing and recognition for their contribution to project success. We work hard to provide this feedback and recognition."

"Lucy, you're talking about more than just setting project principles; you're talking about developing a new work culture, and I can see you need to have a strong base of values. Even though I'm bringing together a team that has worked on a lot of projects and has some preconceived ideas about the culture we'll develop, right now is the time to set the stage for doing business differently. If I'm hearing you correctly, you're suggesting that projects are the prime opportunity to start doing business differently because they do not have an existing culture to replace, but can start from scratch, or as close as they can come to being started from scratch."

"Chris, I know I'm making it sound easy. Some of it is easy, but it still takes a lot of hard work. Sometimes you think it's all hogwash, but if you can get it started and can stick it out, you'll be amazed at the difference."

"Can you give me some other examples of principles you developed on your project?"

"Sure," said Lucy. "Be totally honest with the entire project team. I know this sounds simple, but sometimes we temper information because we believe it might make the project look bad. Another is to maintain complete and honest communication. One principle that may seem strange to you is the involvement of the family whenever possible. John feels particularly strong about the importance of the family and how they are really part of our success."

"I think I see what you are talking about, but these will have to be developed by the entire project management team to get their buy-in. What kind of process did you use, and how long did it take?"

Lucy thought a long time before answering that one. The project team had gone through several meetings that, individually, would have seemed wasteful, but the culmination of all the meetings had built a strong, flexible, and predictable leadership team. Ken had asked all of the members of the leadership team to complete a Myers Briggs Type Indicator.[4] The instrument helped team members to share their own personal characteristics and some things that motivated them, and to understand the characteristics of others.

---

[4]For more information about the MBTI, see Appendix E.

On another occasion, Ken had introduced a Lifeline[5] exercise. In this exercise, team members had charted their life history. It was an excellent tool for getting to know people beyond the one dimension of work. These exercises very quickly created a basis for trust. The culmination of these activities helped develop the project's value base. Even though these had been important to Lucy and her project team, Chris was looking for the short version. What could she offer that would have value for Chris?

"Chris, if I were you, I'd ask Ken to facilitate a half-day session. I think you could devise a basic value statement in that time, but I would ask Ken first."

"What's a basic value statement?" asked Chris.

"It's a statement, developed through consensus, that clarifies the basic values of the project," Lucy responded.

"But you haven't told me what process you used?" insisted Chris. "I want a little more than what you have given me before I start down this path. I sense that this isn't something I can start and then change my mind and go back to my old way of doing business."

"You're right, Chris. Once you start, you can modify and choose between a lot of options, but you'll lose a lot if you bring out that symbolic baseball bat once you've told people you've burned it," Lucy agreed. "The person to talk to is Ken; he can give you options and better feedback on your thoughts."

"Who is Ken, anyway?" asked Chris. "I've seen him at company meetings and know he's involved in our corporate quality program, but what's he doing on your project?"

"That's a question for John Picard," responded Lucy. "Ken is a valuable member of our team; John invited him to join the team before anybody else. So you need to ask John what his thinking was at the time. All I know is that John says he will never manage another major project without someone like Ken."

As CHRIS WALKED TO HIS CAR, he almost wished he hadn't talked to Lucy. This total quality thing was growing stronger in the company, but developing a value base for the project and doing all this psychological stuff? It was too much.

---

[5]The Lifeline exercise is described in more detail in Appendix F.

GLASBERGEN

"We installed little monitors because they make all of our problems seem smaller."

Chris was a successful project manager. He'd never had a project go sour. Still, John Picard was the best; a little on the academic side, but as solid as a rock. As he pondered what Lucy had told him, Chris realized that this felt something like the computer movement. Not that long ago, Chris had been one of the first to use computers on his project, but they hadn't lived up to their billing until his third or fourth project. He'd spent more time fixing computer problems than he did running the project. Eventually, of course, it paid off.

But this was a change in management style, which meant a change in Chris. He wasn't sure he was ready for that. The company was pushing in the total quality direction—but not very hard. His division head hadn't even said a word about it yet, so Chris would be on his own if he were to try this new approach.

What Chris was formulating in his mind was a cost and risk/reward analysis. The risk was the possible failure of the project or a project that performed less well than management expected—and no explanation would help if management was unhappy with the project. The cost could be some sleepless nights.

If my computer analogy is near correct, Chris thought, *this project will take more time and more worry than I want to give. And what if things go wrong? I'll spend so much time at the project, I'll never see the family. That's a big cost AND a big risk. What's the reward? Maybe a better-run project. Why is John Picard and his team selling this so hard? Where's the benefit?*

Maybe it's time to see John.

The only way to win is to fight on the side of your adversaries.
Francis Picabia in Who Knows: Poems and Aphorisms

Chapter 10

"Do I Need a Quality Process Facilitator?"

C HRIS DIDN'T HESITATE. Two days later, he asked John Picard to meet him at Jack's Grill for lunch. Jack's offered a good selection of food and an atmosphere conducive to conversation. Plus, it was within walking distance of the office. The meeting would help Chris make up his mind; if he decided to try this new approach, it would be because John convinced him it was worth both the cost and the risk. Or maybe there was a middle ground. Maybe he could try a few things without risking too much.

After the small talk about the family and old times had worn down, Chris jumped in. "John, I hear you've been successful on this project, even beyond your normal great job. Lucy says you've applied a total quality approach to your project, and it's paying you big dividends. How much of what I'm hearing is true?"

Chris saw the gleam in John's eye and knew he was in for the long version.

"Chris, you wouldn't believe some of the things we've done on this project," John began. "Right now we are 68 percent complete, three months ahead of schedule, and on track to underrun the budget by $22 million on a $200 million dollar project. Not bad for an untried approach."

Chris cut John off before he could get into the details. "Lucy suggested that my next step should be to see Ken. Although I've met Ken and he seems like a pleasant and competent person, I don't see how he fits into your project."

"When I view my job as project manager," John explained, "I have two primary functions: to manage the *technical* side of the project and to manage the *people* side of the project. Geoff McCoy is the leader for managing the technical challenges, and Ken assists me in managing the *people* side. If you believe, as I do, that people are the most important part of a successful effort, then it makes sense to invest and focus effort on that part of the equation."

81

John smiled to himself. He remembered asking Buck Myers these same questions Chris was now asking him. Buck had been the company's vice president in charge of total quality back when "quality" seemed like only a new buzzword. Although he could not provide good reasons, he recommended that John put a full-time "people person" on the project. It was a decision John would never regret, but he still always struggled to define what Ken did that helped a project so much.

In the beginning, Ken had facilitated the focusing workshops and helped the total quality teams get started. He'd participated in the project's progress meetings and client review meetings. He developed and maintained both hard and soft measurements for the project, but even that didn't fully describe what he did. John hadn't realized Ken's impact on the project until Ken went to the company headquarters in Nashville for two weeks and he saw the impact that Ken's absence had on the project. Things became just a little sluggish. Now, Chris was looking for concrete answers, and John knew he just didn't have them.

"Chris, I'll say to you what Buck Myers said to me: 'Trust me and get a full-time process facilitator,'" explained John. "He'll pay your investment back many times over."

"John, I need more than that," Chris pressed him. "How do I write out performance expectations if I don't know what to expect?"

"Okay, Chris," answered John. "In general terms, Ken provides the focus on the big picture. He's always asking 'does this help us achieve our vision?' He provides feedback and advice on team morale and spirit. He also helps me communicate sensitive issues to the team. He's trusted by the team; they see him as their friend on the management team. He's brought tools and techniques for measuring progress and for getting people involved. But most of all, Ken is the project's conscience. His presence reminds us of the way we want to operate. He encourages us to keep looking at our management style and to question if that's the way we want to manage."

John saw Chris' puzzled look. But instead of trying to explain that same concept further, he decided to go all the way and present Chris with another idea that would boggle his mind. He knew that Chris would either accept the concepts John was sharing with him or not— and if not, he shouldn't waste any time. "Ken also helps us have fun— probably the most important contribution to project success," John added with a smile.

"How serious are you?" asked Chris.

"Actually, very serious. We've done some things to keep the project light, like crazy tie day, grubby day and pizza parties at lunch. Ken brought in his son's remote control car and ran it all over the floor. We

82

"I went to work this morning wearing
a great big smile, but my boss said
it was a violation of their dress code."

dressed up on Halloween. Ken is always holding poetry contests and poster contests on the project. I've never enjoyed a project like this one," confessed John.

"You enjoy the project because it is a success," Chris responded.

"You're right, Chris, but it was a success partly *because we had fun.* Remember, this is a high-technology project with a lot of uncertainty. Creativity in our approach is essential for us to be successful. The fun things keep us loose and free-thinking. The worst thing that could happen to us would be to get into a rut or to routinize the project in a way that stifles creativity. You know I'm a firm believer that routine work drives out nonroutine work and thinking, creating and planning can lose out to the routine work of the project, if we let it."

"Okay, John, when can you release Ken from your project?" inquired Chris.

"Sorry, Chris," he shook his head, "you'll need to find someone else. Ken is obligated for nine more months."

"Can you recommend someone who would be good for my project?"

That was a tough one. John couldn't think of anyone else in the company that would fit the bill like Ken. Ken had come to the company after making a significant career change, and his previous experience brought something special to the project. Unlike most of the company's employees, Ken had a degree in social work and had done postgraduate training in psychology. He'd lived abroad for several years, first as a Peace Corps volunteer, then as a social worker for an international relief agency. Back in the States, he'd been the director of several nonprofit agencies. Then he'd made one of those midlife career changes and gone back to school for a master's degree in project management.

After the company hired him, Ken had participated in a nine-month internal project management training program. Ken spent about six weeks in each of the major departments: Project Controls, Project Procurement, Value Engineering, and Project Estimating. He then spent two years on projects before the company transferred him back to headquarters to help develop a Total Quality Management program for projects.

All of those experiences combined had created the perfect candidate for helping projects implement total quality. Ken brought people skills, experience in each of the project's departments, project management education and project experience to John's project.

John finally answered Chris by saying, "The person you select must first have credibility. He—or she—must be seen as a peer by the management team and a leader by the rest of the project team. People must know the quality facilitator has your complete confidence. It must be someone with good people skills and broad project experience. Maybe the hardest quality to find is someone who is willing to take a back seat and give credit to the team for success that is rightfully theirs."

"I'm glad I wasn't held to that criteria when they selected me for this project," Chris joked. Then he got up and shook John's hand. "You've really helped," he said. "I know there are no easy answers, but I feel more comfortable now. Just keep thinking about a good candidate for my project."

There is no limit to what a man can do so long as he does not care a straw who gets the credit for it.

C. E. Montague in Disenchantment

Chapter 11

Focus on Goals, Not Performance

The free way of life proposes ends, but it does not prescribe means.
Robert F. Kennedy in The Pursuit of Justice

C HRIS LESTER WALKED thoughtfully toward Ken's office. He'd made the appointment the day before, but now he wondered what he really wanted to know. Lucy had talked about project principles and values, John had talked about the project being people-focused. Was he heading to Ken's office just to get more of the same? Chris had already decided to add a quality facilitator to the project team even though he wasn't sure what to expect. Maybe Ken could add some clarity.

Ken was drawing on a flip chart when Chris knocked on the door jamb. "Hi, there," Ken turned to shake Chris' hand. "Good to see you again. I heard you got the Webster Project. Congratulations!"

Chris felt Ken's sincerity in the warm handshake. He smiled a response and pointed to the flip chart. "What are you working on?"

"A project SWAT Team is looking for ways to reduce the approval time on requests for proposals from five days to three. I'm revising the work process flowchart from my notes of the meeting."

"From five days to three?" Chris asked incredulously. "The average time to get those approvals in this company is two weeks!"

Ken gave Chris a small but perceptible smile.

Chris had just walked in the office and already felt he had more questions to ask than he had time to ask them. He tried to stay on track. "I'm going to put a quality facilitator on the project management team, and I want your advice on what I should expect and what I need to do to help make this work," Chris said. "But before we get into that, tell me what a SWAT team is, and we'll save how you got the approval process down to five days for another time."

Ken explained that SWAT stood for *Specific Work-process Action Team,* a team designed to help the project focus on a single problem or opportunity. The team usually analyzed the work processes tied to the opportunity or problem and identified actions the project could implement. This kind of team looked for the greatest impact in the shortest time. They had a special personality, because they could start up, solve the problem or improve the process, and then go away.

Ken was explaining how the teams were charted, and his role in assisting them when Chris interrupted, "I want to understand and probably use SWAT teams, especially if I can get approvals in five days, but I've got an interview for a quality facilitator tomorrow, and what I need right now is a better understanding of the role. How can this person best help my project?"

"By helping the project keep goal-focused," Ken answered without hesitation. "Projects by definition have a limited amount of resources. The success of a project is thus tied to how well the project utilizes those resources. By focusing on the things that will have the greatest impact on the project, you will maximize project performance.

"A project that is *too* focused can't react to new information or opportunities. This kind of project finishes ahead of schedule, under budget and meets all the specifications but still has an unhappy client," Ken continued. "Most good managers can focus on one or two dimensions of a project and meet some well defined measurements. The problem arises when projects become more complex and, as you know, most of our projects are increasing in complexity. As complexity increases, project managers need to commit more of the project's energy to understanding and reacting to issues that will impact the project."

"Wait a minute!" Chris interjected. "I understand project energy. That's the resources of the project manager: the sum total of the available skills, talents, enthusiasm and hours of all the people on the project. If I communicate an expectation that members of the project team should expend all their energy on cost and schedule issues, of course they will miss some other key issues. No project manager knows everything they need to know to execute the project from the beginning. Every project develops over time, reacting and changing as we learn more and as the environment in which we execute the project changes. The same goes for the rest of the project's management team. They had better be learning and applying what they learn to their project planning."

"I suppose that's why John Picard refers to a project as a *learning organization,*" Ken nodded reflectively. "He says a learning organization continually searches for new information and grows and reforms itself in response to these new learnings. That's why John says a project manager who tries to manage his current project like his last project has decreasing performance."

86

"John was always a little weird," Chris grinned. "But I like him and you can't knock his performance. His results are some of the best in our business. In fact, I think he's one of the top ten project managers in the world. But when *I* want to talk about improving project schedules, *he* wants to talk about SWAT teams, the power of fun, or learning organizations! Me, I'm just a simple project manager who wants to manage a big, world-class, expensive project. Is that too much to ask?" Chris smiled playfully.

"If life were only so simple!" Ken replied, also smiling. "But some projects are more complex than others and the need for focus or the type of focus varies at different phases of a project."

"Okay, the phases of a project I understand. The beginning of a project is always a time of confusion, since we're bringing a lot of different viewpoints together. Later, as we come to some common understanding and direction, we still search for innovative and creative ways to accomplish the project. But there comes a point where we switch into a *production* mode, where we need to get the work out. Then, some innovations, although creative and maybe good ideas, will actually have a negative impact on the project. The end of a project yet another character. Is this what you mean by the complexity of a project?" Chris asked.

"Not really," answered Ken. "The different phases of a project definitely have different characteristics and the use of goals is a helpful tool for the project management team to help the project transition from one phase to another, but the complexity I'm talking about is a little different.

"When I evaluate the complexity of a project, I look first at the technology," continued Ken. "Is this new technology, a change in existing technology, or is this a 'build-me-one-just-like-the-last-one' technology? I look at the complexity of the contract, the make-up of the decision-making process, how many people are involved, what cultures are involved in the project."

"What about size, duration, risk, clarity of objectives?" asked Chris. "These are issues that really impact a project and the way you manage it."

"Actually, we've developed a list of twenty major issues that significantly impact the complexity of a project," Ken answered. "We call it the *complexity index* and we use it as a tool to evaluate complexity and to determine the appropriate skills we're looking for in a project manager."

Project Complexity Index
C=(Complexity of Item)
P=(Potential Impact on Project)

Project Variables		Very Low	Low	Medium	High	Very High
Technology	P					
	C					
Environment	P					
	C					
Location(s)	P					
	C					
Size	P					
	C					
Duration	P					
	C					
Sponsorship	P					
	C					
Governmental concerns/ issues	P					
	C					
Communication issues	P					
	C					
Legal	P					
	C					
Cultural	P					
	C					
Clarity of objectives	P					
	C					
Risk	P					
	C					
Management support	P					
	C					
Availablity of resources	P					
	C					
Linking mechanisms	P					
	C					
Labor issues	P					
	C					
Contractual complexity	P					
	C					
Organizational structure	P					
	C					
Project management skills and experience	P					
	C					
Project team skills	P					
	C					

Evaluate the commercial philosophy of the project: partnering philosphy, bidding philosophy, incentives, financing, lump sum, cost plus, fixed fee. What is the potential impact of the commercial strategy?

_____
_____
_____
_____

"Okay, I get it." Chris summarized his understanding. "For more complex projects, we're looking for project managers who have better people skills. We look for managers that can tolerate a good deal of ambiguity. Complex projects have multiple variables that must be managed simultaneously. Our project managers must be able to build a responsive organization. A project team has to react to new information, refining or even rebuilding the project plan as new information comes along. I understand how more complex projects need a different management style and probably a different set of project management skills, but we started this discussion on how to use *goals* on my project."

"Because of your experience and your reputation, Chris, you'll be asked to manage more complex projects," Ken said. "On those kind of projects, your challenge is to focus the team on the keys to success without creating a microscopic view that becomes inflexible and unresponsive. Your goal development process is one of your best processes for developing the appropriate focus."

"Let me get this clear," Chris said. "You're saying I can have a well-developed scope, a good relationship with my client, be on schedule and below cost, and *still* miss the boat if I don't have good goal development on my project?"

"No," answered Ken. "Goal development is just one tool, but it's an important tool in managing your project. Let me tell you about my trip to the Oakland Upgrade Project I was asked to visit a couple of months ago."

"Okay," Chris leaned back in his chair. "I've learned to expect a story or two when I'm trying to communicate with You-All from the South—or is it You-*Uns* from the South?"

"Depends which side of the ridge you were born on," Ken responded with a smile. "You've gotten used to Southern ways—only because we don't tell you flat out when you're full of it!"

"Right," Chris grinned. "But, seriously, I have noticed that a lot of people here in the South use stories to communicate a point. It can be distracting when you're in a meeting, but one-on-one, I usually find it's a good way to get concepts and ideas across. So 'y'all go right ahead'!"

Ken monitored the type of humor used among the team members closely, and tried to bring any tendency to use humor in a negative, hurtful way to the attention of the guilty party. But regional jokes were a common link in their highly diversified office, although Ken sometimes worried when the jokes seemed to have a meaner side. On this occasion, he knew this was Chris' way of expressing warmth. So Ken went on with his story.

89

The wit makes fun of other persons; the satirist makes fun of the world; the humorist makes fun of himself, but in so doing, he identifies himself with people—that is, people everywhere, not for the purpose of taking them apart, but simply revealing their true nature.

James Thurber

ONE OF THE CORPORATE VICE PRESIDENTS had asked Ken to visit this particular project. The VP needed to understand some of the negative news that he was hearing. While interviewing members of the project management team, Ken had asked how clear the goals were. They were clear, was the general answer. But when asked what the goals were, a large variety of answers came back. A great deal of work was being done on the project, people were working hard and long hours. Each member of the team focused on the tasks at hand and reacted to issues as they developed. Although each team within the project maximized production and effort, the project's progress did not meet the expectations of the project management team. Communication issues caused rework, critical activities weren't recognized until after they began impacting the project, and the client began asking how such experienced and smart managers could miss such basic project activities.

"So your suggestion was to institute a goal development process?" asked Chris.

"Yes, but the team felt that they had all the tools they needed. They had a schedule that told them they were behind and they knew what activities needed extra effort to catch up. They said *all they needed to do was work harder*." Ken shrugged expressively.

Chris chuckled as he got up and walked toward the door. "Developing goals is easy," he said. "Developing the *right* goals is the trick.

"Sometimes I look at my desk at the end of the day," Chris continued, pausing in the doorway, "and I see fifty things that I worked on and I feel like I would have been better off not coming to work. That's lack of focus. If I had identified the three most important things I needed to get done for the day and accomplished those, I could go home feeling good.

"At the other extreme, there have been days when I am so focused on a task that someone will come in my office and I'm startled when I realize they're there. I was so focused on my work I didn't notice anything. Sometimes that kind of focus is good, but most of the time I'd better be able to know what's going on in my surroundings.

"I guess it's the same thing with a project." Chris continued, thinking out loud. "Your project can get so focused that people are not aware of important information in the environment. On other occasions, everything on the project is important and nothing gets the appropriate management attention."

Chris stood for a moment, deep in thought. Focusing a project was a balancing act. If you created too much focus, a project would fail to react to key issues. Without sufficient focus, each person on the project works on the activities they see as important, reducing the power and synergy of a coordinated team. A good project manager can use project goals to bring the right level of focus to a project.

Chris realized the conversation was not really over. He returned to his seat across from Ken. "John and I talked about a Focusing Workshop, where we define what's important to the customer. I believe in the company's definition of a total quality project as a project that understands, manages, and meets the customer's expectations. I know how the Focusing Workshop helps us understand expectations and begins the planning process for meeting those expectations. This sounds like a real improvement to our traditional scope-defining meetings. Those are like the starting point for developing the project goals. The Focusing Workshop then focuses the project on the success *of the client*. The project management goals focus the management team on the project success and the division goals focus and communicate key success factors to the entire team."

Ken began describing how each manager within the project aligns his or her portion of the project with the overall project vision and key goals, but Chris interrupted, "Geoff McCoy already explained how his technical group developed a vision statement, and so on, but there's got to be more ...?"

"The project remains focused throughout the goal development process," Ken responded. "Short-term goals, usually monthly, are developed by each major division of the project. These goals support the overall goals of the project. From the project level we ask, what are the goals we need to achieve next month to keep the project on track, to move toward achieving our vision and key goals? This isn't an easy process. Teams sometimes have significant disagreement on what the goals need to be. Goal-setting meetings provide a forum where the team

91

discusses its priorities and allocation of resources, which always means compromise. I have seen these discussions become *very* heated. But they need to take place and the project manager needs to make sure they take place.

"Each division then adds more detail so that the division understands the goals they must achieve to support the project's goals," Ken continued. "This process keeps flowing throughout the project until everybody associated with the project knows what goals they must achieve to keep the project goals on track."

"This sounds like a work breakdown structure used for developing the project schedule," Chris remarked.

"Very similar," Ken agreed. "Although goals can include work activities, they are usually broader in nature. My rule of thumb is that everybody on the project has three goals they need to achieve during each week to support their division's goals."

KEN THEN TOOK CHRIS ON A TOUR of the project's work area, randomly selecting members of the team to share with Chris their weekly goals. Most were posted on walls or desktops with progress highlighted in bright colors.

Chris noticed that each team member had the division's goals, but also had one or more "stretch" goals attached. He learned, by asking people, that stretch goals were goals that would normally be done the next month, but if it made sense and a team member could work on them, they would be done this month.

A chart was on the main wall by the exit for everybody to see. The chart had most of the goals marked off and many of the stretch goals were marked complete. In addition, the charts had celebration plans listed for that month, and several months in advance. This prompted Chris to ask a young technician close to the door what those celebration plans were for.

"The celebrations are for exceeding each month's goals," she answered.

"I see Groundhog Barbecue listed as the celebration in February. Is that what you're working toward?" asked Chris in disbelief.

"In a way," answered the technician. "You see, the technical manager came from Pennsylvania, somewhere near where that groundhog-shadow thing takes place, you know? Anyway, he thought it would be a good idea for celebrating January's successes and Groundhog Day at the same time.

"You see," she went on, "it's also a casual day. The company's pretty tight about the dress code, you know, dress for success and all that. If you want to be a manager, you wear suits a lot. However, when we celebrate, we ignore the code and wear jeans and sweaters. It makes it a special day and the atmosphere is a lot looser. Some of the most creative work is done on casual days.

"The other thing about a casual day," she continued, "is that everybody else *knows* we're celebrating. People see that this is a special project and that we're being successful. Geoff McCoy, our manager, will serve the entire team barbecue."

The technician saw the blank look in Chris Lester's eyes and knew she had to explain the obvious.

"You see, the reward itself isn't what's important, although we do have a good time. It's the *celebration* of success that's the main thing. It's kind of like celebrating the Super Bowl. The celebration doesn't just acknowledge the success you just achieved—it's also about enjoying the accomplishment and knowing you did something great. That's what gears you up to go after your next goal. You want to keep that feeling of specialness."

"But doesn't it get old? Eating barbecue and casual day?" asked Chris.

"That's where you find the managers on this project getting real creative. This month's celebration will be Turkey Day. I heard some of these cutups are planning Pilgrim and Indian costumes. You never know around here, with these guys!"

As Chris and Ken walked back to Ken's office, Ken explained how celebrations became an important part of keeping the project focused. Goals and measurements were developed and the periodic celebrations reaffirmed to everyone associated with the project that they were on track.

When they got back to Ken's office, Ken gave Chris a celebration checklist. He explained that celebrations had to be taken seriously and that the wrong type of celebrating could be as harmful as the right kind is beneficial. The key was to select the right goals, the right measurements, and then celebrate in the right way.

"Have you got a few more minutes?" Chris asked.

Ken sat down and leaned forward to give Chris his undivided attention.

"I can see how the goal development process keeps the project on track and how celebrations are an important part of the process, but how do you find measurements that let you know that you're doing what you think you're doing?

93

Ken's Celebrations Checklist

✓ Celebrate in the work area.
✓ Display measurements of success (why we are celebrating).
✓ Discuss the value of the success to the project.
✓ Discuss what we did to be successful.
✓ Celebrate within one week of the accomplishment.
✓ Invite client to speak.
✓ Invite corporate sponsor to speak.
✓ Make level of celebration commensurate with level of accomplishment.
✓ Do not discuss future goals.
✓ Verbal reinforcement must be sincere, specific to the accomplishment and personal.

"I remember the Pulliam Project," Chris continued. "We measured *everything* on that project. Marissa Lavone, the Nashville general manager, kept saying, 'If you can't measure it, you can't improve it.' We invested so much time in measurement and we didn't know any more than if we hadn't measured a thing. Still worse was the impact it had on the team. Everybody was looking for new ways to find someone doing something wrong. I don't want to get into that again."

Ken understood Chris' concerns. He'd seen a number of projects get lost because they had either too much, not enough, or the wrong kind of measurements. Ken pulled out some measurement guidelines for Chris and explained the two principal kinds of measurement they were using on John's project.

The first were used to track project goals. These measurements provided data and helped determine if progress was being made toward the goals. "Traditional cost and scheduling measurements fall into this category," Ken explained. "Other measurements may need to be developed to measure key goals of the project. For example, if a project goal is to develop good supplier relationships, then the project should develop a measurement for that, such as a survey for tracking that relationship. These goals and measurements are interrelated. Developing goals and developing measurements used to be separate processes. Project teams were asked to define their charter, then establish their goals, then develop measurements for tracking the goals.

94

After each step, the team brought the results back to the management team for review. This review allowed the management team to reaffirm the team's direction or to make small corrections if the team was off track a little. The review also allowed the management team to reinforce the process at intervals—not just when the team had finished.

"But the project team discovered that the development of goals and the development of measurements was a symbiotic process; that the team would discuss goals for a while, then switch to measurements, then back to goals until both goals and measurements took on form. We changed the process so that teams now define their charter, and then develop goals and measurements *simultaneously*."

Ken continued to explain that their experience indicated that, because every project was unique, the goals were therefore unique, and that the measurements almost always needed to be developed as the goals for the project were established. They could not rely on pulling measurement tools off the company's shelf for use on the project.

"What about the measurements you were showing on the flowcharts when I first came to your office?" Chris asked.

"The second kind of measurements we use on the project measure work processes," answered Ken. "This is where your statement 'If you can't measure it, you can't improve it' comes in. We focus on opportunities that have a good-size impact on the project or problems that may have a negative impact on the project and analyze them carefully. Many times this involves measurements. Remember the number of days for approval that you were amazed at when you first came into my office? That's the kind of measuring we do to understand the work process and know if we are improving."

Chris looked up from taking notes and noticed that Ken had finished. It all made sense, nothing surprising in the discussion, but Chris knew that things sometimes sounded easy but were tough to implement. He asked, "What is your performance factor on the project?"

"I don't know," answered Ken.

"Could you find out for me?"

"No. We're not keeping the performance factor on this project."

Chris' mouth fell open. The performance factor was the company's measure of all projects. It was sacrosanct. Every project in the company measured their performance against the project estimate. A performance factor (PF) of 1 indicated the performance was exactly what was estimated. If the project, function or even a person fell below 1, they tended to get a lot of negative management attention. A PF above 1 meant that managers left you in peace.

"I'm up for my very first performance review this week.
I'm going to sing a song from 'Cats'."

Chris knew that technical people frequently became masters at manipulating their reports so that they always got a PF of 1, or very near to it. If they were performing a little less than expected, they hid the data, thinking they could catch up before someone caught on. Sometimes they could hide the true data until near the end of the project, hoping that they would have moved on before the true picture was understood.

At the other extreme, Chris remembered working on a project several years ago with an exceptionally bright technical expert. That guy would focus on his work for a week or two at a time, working hard and smart. Even though he didn't work overtime, he would get ahead of schedule by a week or two. Then he would lay back and relax, sneaking out for long lunches, leaving early from work, reading newspapers and books at his desk. If anybody checked up, he pulled out that extra work done weeks before and submitted it like he had just done it that day.

As Chris thought about those two extremes, he knew the performance factor was a poor way to measure performance, an imperfect tool, but that was about all they had. Now Ken was saying they had even thrown that away.

Chris said, "You're telling me the only mechanism you used on a $250 million project for measuring performance is this goal-tracking process?"

96

"Yes!" Ken stated proudly. "If you select the right goals, determine the right measurements, and recognize people for achieving their goals, you can keep the project on track."

Chris considered this. True, he'd always hated this part of a project: trying to make sure no one was cheating, trying to see through the games to truly understand if the project was really on schedule. If Ken's process worked, and he could get his upper management's permission, it would be worth the investment.

But Chris wanted to make sure he understood this process. "Reinforcing people as they achieve their goals will keep the project on track?"

Ken nodded, adding, "The development of goals and measurements is just as important because if you reinforce the wrong things you could end up taking the project in the opposite direction from what you wanted. If you have time, let me share another short war story with you."

"You get what you reinforce."

Ken told the story of his trip to the Parkersburg office a couple of years before. The prime attribute of the project managers in Parkersburg seemed to be their ability to handle a crisis. The office had had so many projects go into a crisis situation that they needed project managers who could put recovery plans together and keep their heads when a project began suffering setbacks. Ken was told that the best crisis managers in the company headed for Parkersburg, because there, they were needed and appreciated. All their top project managers had reputations for handling a crisis.

Then Ken talked to another Parkersburg project manager, Steve. Steve had a different view of the situation. He always seemed to get the easy projects, the ones where the customer was easy to get along with, and the project stayed on schedule and within budget with very few problems. But Steve had explained to Ken that the manager who proved he could manage a crisis was recognized in the Parkersburg office as the premier manager. They were the ones who got the bonuses and were first to be promoted. So what many managers tended to do was *create a manageable crisis*. They would create problems that they knew they could solve and that would make them heroes! Steve refused to play this game. His projects were no easier than any other project of

"Productivity is way up this quarter.
Our department is producing
25% more mistakes, 42% more excuses,
and 58% more paper clip bracelets."

that size and complexity, but instead of good crisis management skills, Steve applied good planning skills. He didn't get much recognition, but he had a loyal team.

"And you checked this out?" asked Chris.

"Yes, and I got confirmation from several people."

"I guess I'm not too surprised. It sounds like some of the games we played in the Boston office," Chris snorted.

"Well, the point I'm trying to make is that if you reinforce poor planning by rewarding it, that's what you get. But by the same token, you can reinforce creativity and get more of it."

"Okay. Well, I came in here looking for a profile for the quality facilitator for my project. I guess I'll have to add 'must be able to develop goals and measurements and reinforce the right things.' Does this person really exist?"

Ken gave Chris that same enigmatic little smile. "John Picard seems to think so."

They both laughed as Chris headed for his next appointment. He almost started to jog down the hall, because he was going to be late. He was spending so much time trying to understand this total quality stuff, it was getting hard to get his job done. He wondered if it would really be worth it.

E Mail, sent 11/15, 13:21; fr: C. Lester to: K. Troy. Ref: 2343892. Priority C, Delivered 11/15, 13:29.

Ken,
I have been trying to develop an acronym to help the team remember some criteria for developing goals. How about SCRAM: Specific, Customer focused, Realistic, Affirmative, and Measurable.

If I remember our discussion goals need to be specific enough to be well understood, measurable, not just good ideas, realistic, not pie-in-the-sky, affirmative, measure where we are going, NOT where we don't want to go. We also agreed that our goals need to be timeframed but I can't find a place for a "t". Maybe SMART GOALS. Specific, Measurable, Affirmative, Realistic and Timeframed, But now I lose the customer. Do you have an acronym I can use??????

Chris

E Mail, sent 11/15, 13:21, fr: C. Lester to: K. Troy. Ref: 2343892. Priority C, Delivered 11/15, 13:29..REPLY 11/15, 15:22

Chris,
Sorry, you've done better than I could. Just pick one and go.
Ken

— Memo —

To: John Picard

cc: Ken Troy

From: Chris Lester   *C.L.*

Date: November 20

Subject: Personal Thanks

Just wanted you to know I brought a project process facilitator on board yesterday. I hired Barbara Hill, a person with a human resources background and skills that seem similar to Ken's. Ken has agreed to help develop our TQM plan for the project and facilitate the Focusing Workshop. Ken will also coach Barb through her first month as a process facilitator.

We had our first celebration yesterday. It was fun and we have began creating the atmosphere you predicted.

Thanks again for all your help and for the loan of Ken.

Chapter 12

Motivation: Who Steers the Boat?

*Surround yourself with the best people you can find, delegate authority,
and don't interfere.*

Ronald Reagan

KEN WAS ABOUT to fall asleep at his desk. Early afternoons were always hard for him. *If I were on vacation*, he thought, *I'd be enjoying an afternoon nap right now.* Ken's vacation routine seldom varied. With his wife, Dawn, vacations meant early runs on the beach, mid-morning coffee overlooking the ocean, noon swimming and an afternoon nap. This schedule always left lots of energy for candlelight dinners and dancing. That late afternoon quiet time was the key to balancing his energy.

Ken knew how he functioned best and right now his biological clock said "take a rest," but his work clock said "no way." Even though Ken was famous for challenging the system and getting away with it, for questioning rules that didn't make sense to him, he knew that an afternoon nap would stretch the tolerance of even the most opened-minded managers. He was attempting to kick his brain back in gear when Chris Lester walked into his office and initiated what turned out to be an interesting conversation.

"Ken, I've just spent the last two hours with Dave Gilbert. He's as good as they come. I've heard about him for years," Chris began. "If you remember, he was one of those who got special recognition at the technical convention in Orlando last January. I was pleased as punch when he agreed to be part of the project leadership team. Now I'm not so sure."

Ken waited as Chris collected his thoughts.

"Dave just told me a story about when he was a kid. He said he used to have about ten of these small self-propelled boats that he played with in a lake. He would line them up and start them across the lake one at a time, trying to get them to reach the other side at the same place. The key, according to Dave, was to make sure the boat started straight and then quickly correct any moves off course.

"He was using this story to explain his management philosophy," continued Chris. "He said, just like his boats, people come with different strengths. You make sure you spend enough time at the start to get the boat heading the right direction and make corrections early. The skill, according to Dave, is to keep track of all your boats and spend time on the ones that stray farthest from the course. If a boat takes too much time, you remove it from the lake, because the other boats will fail to finish because you spent too much time on that one boat."

Again, Ken sat quietly as Chris thought.

"Dave has the clout to get the best people in the company," Chris went on. "He's a winner and people are attracted to him. I know he'll do his part of the project as good as it can be done." Then Chris added, in a distressed tone, "but if he has so much to offer my project, why do I have this feeling that he's the one member of the project leadership that will prevent me from creating the kind of project I envision?"

Ken knew Chris was using this discussion to explore his own feelings. He didn't want instant answers, just a place to find his own answers and Ken's office provided that kind of place.

"Tell me more about what you're feeling," Ken suggested. "What did you hear from Dave that concerns you?"

"Don't get me wrong, Ken," Chris said quickly. "I like Dave! He has the most effective use of humor I have ever seen. He can give people a very difficult message in a way that makes it easy to accept. He's a good listener. He knows how to defuse tense situations."

Then Chris smiled wryly. "Yet, if he's so good, why am I here, right?"

Ken smiled. "You tell me."

Chris sighed. "Okay. What makes me uncomfortable is the boat story." He hesitated a minute, then said forcefully. "Let me tell you my philosophy. You get the boats to the other shore by providing a beacon. Each boat has the capacity to determine their own course. My job is to provide the beacon, the light at the end of the journey that shines during good weather and bad."

Chris looked at Ken to gauge his reaction. "That came out a little stronger than I meant it, maybe."

"Maybe not," Ken shrugged. "But why do you feel the beacon is a better analogy?"

"Because we need to *pull* not *push*," Chris explained. "If the boats are truly self-directing, they'll get there faster on their own than if someone is correcting each boat individually."

Chris got up and paced thoughtfully around the room. Finally he turned back to Ken. "Let's talk about people, not boats. If we provide the overall goals of the project, and do a good job communicating these, then people will respond. Remember the discussion we had on tapping into the discretionary effort of the project team?" Chris asked. "We focused on the team, we celebrated team goal attainment, we put our trust in people and then removed barriers that prevented them from achieving their goals. Ken, as good as Dave is, he *cannot* manage a major project that way. There are too many pieces for him to stay on top of it all. I know Dave can manage *his* part of the project very successfully with this philosophy—he's proven that in the past. My problem is, how will he fit in as a key member of the project leadership team? Can he maximize his part of the project and also maximize the entire project? That's where my gut is saying 'watch out.'"

Ken paraphrased back to Chris what he'd heard him say. This gave Chris a chance to hear it again and also let him know that Ken had truly understood the key points. When he did this, Chris knew Ken was focused on his issue.

Ken finished by advising him, "Trust your gut. It's been right more times than wrong; but don't respond based solely on your gut. Use those feelings to explore why you're reacting this way. Chris, you have a big dilemma here," continued Ken. "You're asking one of the most successful managers in the company to change the way he manages, to trust you and take a risk. You've got to ask yourself: *Why would anybody be willing to do that?*"

"Remember John's baseball analogy? You can't steal second base unless you take your foot off first!" Chris responded. "I want to take my project to the next level. I want to make quantum changes in the way we execute, and I can't do that if the key project managers believe that they can achieve all the challenges of this project just by working harder or longer. If there's any place you've got to work *smarter,* not harder, it's on this project!"

"So where are you with all this?" asked Ken.

"Well, I know I've focused on Dave, but it's not just Dave. I have the best managers in the company on my project. Each manager knows their part of the project. They develop and execute plans, solve problems, and write articulate reports. When needed, they pull in the special resources to handle the tricky problems because they have relationships with all the key resources inside and outside the company. In other words, they're all high performers, hand-picked to lead the most complex and critical project in the company. All this—yet I feel like I'm failing."

Chris sat thinking for a minute, frustration growing in his expression. At last he said, "I have the best opportunity of anybody in the company to prove my stuff, I have everything I need, and it's not coming together." He took a deep breath and focused his gaze on Ken. "Okay! Enough self pity. I need to *do* something. I'm not here to cry on your shoulder. I'm here to develop a plan."

"Okay, Chris, what do you want this plan to do?"

"I want a project like John's," answered Chris immediately. "I want the magic John produced. I want people to say that this was the best project they've ever worked on."

Ken nodded, but said nothing. His silence encouraged Chris to continue.

"You know, I went to a project management symposium in New Orleans recently. A record number of project managers attended that annual conference—the membership of the organization has grown by something close to 100 percent in just over a year. Something's happening in this field, Ken. John and I talked about the conference that same organization had in Atlanta fifteen years ago. That conference was dominated by construction people, you didn't see any women and all the workshops were about controlling cost, meeting schedules and project specifications. This year was different, not only in who attended, but the focus of the conference. The discussions were about leadership, motivating people, aligning the project goals with the business needs of the project. The project managers were younger and computer-literate. They thought about and talked about executing projects around the globe. The technology now exists to instantly communicate with any supplier in the world. Project management is changing, just like the world is changing. Customers are demanding shorter development times, they want flexible organizations that can react to a shifting business environment. They want to be able to react, to pull the resources together to do a task and have those resources go away until they are needed again.

"They want the attributes and advantages of projects, they want the skills, tools and techniques we have developed and they want the products we can deliver."

Chris leaned forward and continued excitedly, "At the same time, project management is moving into a new era. We are learning to tap into the incredible energy of the empowered worker. We are finding innovative, caring and motivated people. We are finding that the biggest obstacle to people's investment in our projects is *us*. We get in the way! John's project proves that addressing these soft issues produces hard results. That a new generation of project managers is emerging and even though I probably only have a couple of projects left before I retire, I want to be part of this new phenomenon.

"I look at my project and see all the ingredients. I see innovative thinkers, experienced people with a proven track record. I see a potential that I have not been able to tap into. We are very quickly going about the tasks we always do and if I don't do something and do it fast, the project will develop its own life and I will be stuck managing project problems rather than leading a new kind of project team."

After several minutes of silence Chris asked, "What do you think, Ken? Can I create that magic?"

"You may want to talk with John," suggested Ken.

"I did," Chris shot back, "and he said talk to you. He said every project has unique characteristics and that what worked for him may not be the best for me, that you could help me develop the magic for my project. That was his word: *magic*. I'm here and I'm asking 'now what?'"

Ken asked, "What did Dave say when you discussed this?"

Chris looked away for a minute before replying, "We really haven't discussed it. Dave has some real issues on his part of the project. He's still pulling his team together. His schedule is weak. We've never worked in that part of the world. He ..."

Chris stopped in mid sentence. "I don't really know what he thinks, nor any of the other members of the team. Being focused on project tasks is part of the problem—but more likely I can't ask good people to trust me and do business differently when I don't know myself what it will take or if I have the skills it takes to make it work."

"Chris, it's a vision," said Ken gently. "If you share where you want to go and talk about how you want to get there and asked them to help, they'll make it work. I know Dave, and I know most of the other members of your team. If they accept your vision and have your support, then the 'magic' will happen."

"They may be too busy," Chris said. "This kind of conversation takes time and a lot of energy. It's something we *should* have done upfront." He hesitated a minute and then added, "I'll talk with them individually and if I get some interest, I'll pull the team together. We'll jointly make a project decision on how we want to manage this project.

"If we get that far, I want you to help Barb facilitate that meeting. I want to be sure everyone is a full and equal participant in the meeting. This truly needs to be a team decision," Chris declared.

"No problem!" said Ken. "It sounds like the kind of meeting I enjoy: high energy, creative and focused on the important issues—the *soft* issues," he stressed, and they both laughed.

As CHRIS GOT UP TO LEAVE, Ken added, "If we have your meeting, you can do one more thing to help make it successful."

"What's that?"

"Bring some of Susan's chocolate chip cookies," answered Ken with a smile.

"You've got a deal!"

Chris kept his smile about Ken's last comment all the way down the hall. Susan's chocolate cookies had become a symbol around the office. Nobody was sure how the symbolism got started or for that matter what it really meant, but whenever things got tense, someone would say "relax and have a chocolate chip cookie" and that would break the tension. He and his wife Susan had one of those relationships that just worked. Susan supported Chris in his profession and gave him a lot of positive energy and Chris returned that energy in his support of Susan. Chris would need that support now, he felt. He was moving into an uncomfortable world and would question the wisdom of this decision many times before his confidence took over the process.

Eating is not merely a material pleasure. Eating well gives a spectacular joy to life and contributes immensely to goodwill and happy companionship. It is of great importance to the morale.

Elsa Schiaparelli in Shocking Life

Chapter 13

Sharing Information Empowers People

A change in the weather is sufficient to recreate the world and ourselves.

Marcel Proust in Remembrance of Things Past

L ATE ONE TUESDAY afternoon what would probably be that winter's only snow began to fall. People began leaving the office, afraid they wouldn't get home because of the roads—or maybe just taking advantage of a good excuse to go home and play in the rare Southern snowstorm.

Lucy was thinking of leaving, too. Her husband Paul had already called to remind her to stop at the store for extra bread and milk on the way home.

"I don't know why," she'd joked. "We're not likely to get snowed in for more than a couple of hours!"

Paul had just laughed. "It's a Southern tradition, Lucy. It's required."

Lucy smiled to herself as she began gathering up her things to leave. Her relationship with Paul allowed her to actively pursue her career because they shared child care responsibilities and household chores and he was always supportive. They tried to take long weekends together as often as possible and to find ways to let each other know how much they appreciated their relationship.

As she turned off her office lights, she thought she'd better just stop by John's office to let him know she was leaving a little early.

John looked up from his desk with a harried expression. "Lucy! I'm glad you're here. I want to talk to you about something. Geoff just left and he was a little upset. It seems he was here until nine o'clock last night and wanted to go home early today but couldn't because he's behind in his paperwork. Geoff thinks we have too many meetings, too many memos, too much paper; in short, he believes we communicate *too* much. We send each other so much information, he says, that it's a full-time job keeping up with the information flow."

John continued, "But Danny was in my office yesterday complaining about a problem that the client had mentioned, but no one had told Danny about. Now he has egg on his face and wants to make sure it doesn't happen again. One manager has a serious problem because we don't communicate enough and another because we communicate too much. Too many meetings waste energy and resources; not having enough and letting a couple of problems like Danny's slip by could put us in deep yogurt."

"John, I think you've always balanced the project against too much or too little communication, and you know I've always encouraged the project to err on the 'too much' side if we're not sure," Lucy said. "You routinely ask people to review the information they receive and inform someone if they don't need or want the information they're receiving. Our meetings are about as efficient as they can get!"

"I appreciate your support, Lucy," John replied quietly, "but what I really need right now is your help in analyzing our communications on our project."

Lucy sighed and pulled up a chair. She knew she would not be going home early. John was looking for someone to bounce ideas off and Lucy knew she handled that well.

Three Kinds of Meetings

She and John began with the project's meeting schedule. The management team had three basic meetings. First, they looked at the *weekly planning meeting*, during which the team spent two hours planning items that were one to three months out. Team members submitted items they believed needed some planning time, and the team focused on what was needed for each of these items. They looked at the long-range project goals as well as the plan to get there, making adjustments where needed. This was a meeting that could not be dropped because it was the only time that, as a team, they withdrew from the day-to-day needs of the project to focus on a more strategic view.

Next, they reviewed the *weekly action item meeting,* during which the project management team checked on their team goals and made recovery plans where necessary. Each functional manager then gave an update on how his or her function was doing against monthly goals.

The third agenda item at this meeting, "action items review," allowed the team to update the action item log. The action item log listed every major activity that was not part of the team goals, the manager responsible for that activity, and when it was to be completed. Action items came out of the planning meeting, from managers identifying actions that needed to be done in the next few weeks, and from the action-item meeting itself. Lucy and John could see no reason to change this format.

John was resolute in his defense of the third type of meeting, the *Friday meeting*. Although they were actually held every other Friday, these meetings were the only ones that did not have an agenda, where John did not lead the meeting, and where almost everything was open for discussion. Friday meetings allowed team members to get things off their chests. If someone didn't like the way something was going, this provided a time to talk about it. It was the one place where the team members could let their hair down. Some of these meetings could get pretty emotional, sometimes they were funny, and sometimes they were just "bull sessions," but John felt they were essential for the team to continue working smoothly. That's why he refused to consider giving them up, although after the first few months of the project, he cut them back to every other Friday.

All other meetings were set as needed to deal with essential issues and problem solving.

Through their discussion, Lucy and John came to agree that the meeting structure of the project was doing what it was designed to do. The conversation needed to head elsewhere so Lucy took the lead.

"Why are you so concerned about communication, John? You communicate information that most project managers consider too sensitive to share with the team and this sharing builds trust with team members.

"In every interaction we have, we communicate a lot, whether we plan to or not. Sometimes silence can communicate all kinds of messages," Lucy continued. "By our actions, choice of words, and the way we interact as a management team and with the project team, we communicate respect, confidence, appreciation, enthusiasm, as well as all kinds of data that the team uses to interpret the subtleties of the project. I'm not worried about these messages because they have always confirmed that we see team members as partners and problem-solvers. The team members solve a myriad of problems very inventively and would not be as proactive without this free sharing of information.

"Remember the Hickory Project that we did for the Goodbody Corporation? Information was so valuable, it became a commodity to be traded. Official information was scarce, so informal information was traded on a kind of black market. A tremendous amount of energy was spent building networks where you could trade information. The more information you had, the better edge you had in your planning and your ability to react. People with a good deal of information were perceived to have power. The more information, the more power. I remember one manager who wouldn't even share information he received in staff meetings because he didn't want his staff to have as much power as he did!

"John," Lucy concluded, "you have always said sharing information is the basis of empowering people and you've lived by those guidelines."

John had listened carefully to Lucy, as he always did, but he still felt uncomfortable. "I'm concerned about information overload," John said with conviction. "Geoff has a point. Sometimes people meet out of habit and put out reports just because that's what they did on their last project. I want to spend a couple of weeks prioritizing our communications. Do our meetings, memos, reports and every other kind of communication focus on communicating what's *important*? Do they communicate our goals first, our plans to achieve those goals second, and then, how we are doing against those plans?"

"That would focus management communications *to* the team, but what about communications *from* the team; problems, problem-solving activities, new ideas, things like that?" asked Lucy.

"I'm not trying to inhibit any communications, Lucy," John responded. "I just want us to be a little more crisp in what we say, efficient in the way we say it, while at the same time making sure we say the things we should. This shouldn't be an excuse for hiding problems—just the opposite, in fact."

> *A fact is like a sack—it won't stand up if it's empty. To make it stand up, first you have to put in it all the reasons and feelings that caused it in the first place.*
> *Luigi Pirandello in* Six Characters in Search of an Author

JUST THEN, GEOFF CAME IN the door, obviously agitated. Both John and Lucy knew Geoff seldom made unplanned trips to anyone's office. He structured his time; if he needed something from you or if he had something you needed, he wrote it down and brought it up at the staff meeting. If it was important enough, he made an appointment. If Geoff arrived without an appointment, it was important, or he was mad.

It didn't take long to find out what was on Geoff's agenda. His anger showed in his posture, face, and the tone of his voice. Lucy got up to leave so they could talk but Geoff motioned her to sit back down. "You might as well hear this too, Lucy."

"For the past three days, whenever I've gone over to Patty Jones' office to see if the Morgan contract was complete, she's been on the telephone on a personal call. I hear her talking about her kids. It's snowing outside, I want to go home early, and I can't leave because I've got to approve this contract and she can't get it done for her personal business. John, you've got to do something!"

John was slow to respond, which was typical. The more tense the situation, the more John seemed to slow down. He seemed to know that the pace of his response would have an impact on the emotion in the air. So, although Geoff was still fidgety, he realized John was intentionally giving him time to think.

"Let me make sure I understand what you're saying." John rephrased Geoff's complaint, a technique called "reflective listening" that he insisted on explaining to everyone he worked with. He believed that repeating back what someone said to you, especially in anger, helped to avoid misunderstanding and defuse emotion.[6]

"Patty Jones is preparing a contract that needs your approval and the contract is not complete but Patty—at least when you've been there—has been attending to personal business instead of project business. This not only impacts the project but costs you personal time that you could better spend in other ways."

Geoff nodded.

"Since Patty works for Danny and not you, you've brought the issue to me. Am I close? " asked John.

"That's about the size of it," answered Geoff tersely.

"What do you need from me?" asked John.

"Talk to Danny and fix the problem," responded Geoff with an impatient gesture.

John thought a minute. Then he suggested, "Since Patty works for Danny, *they* will need to work out a solution. Danny needs to know the details. It would seem better to me if you had this discussion with Danny."

---

[6] Reflective listening techniques are discussed in Appendix G.

Geoff started to reply, but stopped himself and sat quietly for a moment. Finally, he sighed. "I think Danny and I can handle this, John. I was pretty upset and I wanted you to fire Patty. I guess I know that's not the solution. Danny and I will work on it. Sorry to interrupt."

"Geoff," John smiled, "I continue to be amazed at the way you quickly pick up on things, even when you're angry."

"I'll wait and talk to Danny tomorrow. Right now, I think I'll go home and get the sled out of the attic," said Geoff.

"You have a sled?" Lucy asked wide-eyed, as though he was talking about a rare painting.

"Remember I come from Calgary, where a sled is never put in the attic," said Geoff as he headed for the door. He waved goodbye and said, "I'll see you tomorrow—*if* the office is open. Who knows, we could get lucky and have a whole inch of snow."

After Geoff had gone, Lucy smiled at John. "How would that discussion fit into your priority list?"

John shrugged. "People complicate the best-laid plans!"

"No, seriously. Do you think your prioritizing of communications issues will solve Geoff's problem?" asked Lucy.

"I'm not trying to solve a specific problem," answered John. "I'm trying to set some communication principles that will guide the way the project focuses on issues and communication. Our communication should reflect our project principles. It should be goal-directed, client-focused, and people-oriented. If we keep this in mind on everything we do, we will find the right level of communication. We can't set any rules that will answer all the problems. The one rule that comes closest is 'empower people, and they will get the job done.'"

John glanced out the window and then back at Lucy, who still had her coat and briefcase near at hand. "I like this snow too; what do you say we both go home before it starts melting?"

For the happiest life, days should be rigorously planned, nights left open to chance.

Mignon McLaughlin

Communication seems to be a touchy issue on all projects, maybe in every human endeavor. Ken says we are doing a good job, but still, so many problems could be prevented if people just communicated better. Meetings are one area where I have some control. I've spent a lot of time and energy structuring meetings to meet the needs of the project team. I've worked on project procedures and a project environment that encourages—no, expects—good communication.

So why did this episode happen with Geoff today? He's a skilled listener and a patient manager, yet he was ready to jump all over Patty Jones. He actually wanted her fired. Of course, later we all realized he had gotten only part of the story; he hadn't stopped to find out that Patty's child is in the hospital!

Was this a communication problem?

No matter how hard I try, some communication that **needs** to take place doesn't happen. Ken says that I need to balance the energy I put into preventing problems with the possible outcomes when communications are missed. I try to focus on areas where communications are essential and set the right tone on the project. Then I need to patiently deal with the Patty Jones-type issues when they pop up.

Chapter 14

"The Lester Challenge"

Whatever there be of progress in life comes not through adaptation but through daring ...

Henry Miller in The Wisdom of the Heart

D ANNY TURNED A corner in the seventh floor hallway and saw an excited group, including Geoff, crowding around the window. "What's up?" Danny asked him.

"Chris Lester is getting ready to swim the lake!"

"In February!" Danny almost screamed. "Is he crazy?"

"No—haven't you heard? His project met some incredibly difficult milestone, and he's swimming the lake on a bet. Well, maybe not exactly a bet. Yesterday at lunch Wayne Hart, the technical leader on Lester's project, told me the story behind the 'Lester Challenge.'"

Geoff repeated the story to Danny.

AFTER EVERYBODY HAD RETURNED from the Christmas holidays and started reviewing project schedules, it had become obvious that the project could never meet its January milestone goals. The whole project management team had been emotionally down and grumpy.

Then Wayne took up the challenge. He'd assured everyone not to worry; that his team would meet all the milestone goals by January 31st. When pressed to explain how he planned to perform this miracle, Wayne just said, "We'll get it done." At some point, Chris Lester had remarked that if Wayne's team could meet the milestone goals, he would swim the lake in front of the office building.

Not much was made of Chris' offhand comment at the time, but shortly after that meeting, Wayne appointed a quality team and elaborated on what he began to call "The Lester Challenge." He challenged the team to make Chris swim, and the team took up the challenge. Soon posters appeared on the wall announcing the Challenge. All the lead managers were asked to pledge what they could to meet the challenge and quality teams were developed everywhere to find ways to reduce time and meet the goals. The project took on the atmosphere of getting ready for a big game.

114

"Our big project was a great success! We saved the company from ruin and now it's time to celebrate—meet me in the cafeteria for stewed groundhog on toast!"

Chris had seen what was happening. He'd wanted the team to succeed and did little, unobtrusive things to help. *If the team could make the January milestone*, he'd thought, *it would be worth a five-minute swim in freezing water ... maybe*. Anyway, he couldn't have asked for better morale on the project.

A big "thermometer" chart was displayed on the project wall and progress toward the goals posted three times a day. As the deadline got closer, it began to look like the team might reach its goals and their efforts increased. With two days left, the team had worked all night to complete their goals by noon on the last day of the month. Wayne had gathered everybody around and called Chris in as he posted the last activity. Cheers and laughter had erupted as they set the date for the swim and then, with a satisfied feeling of accomplishment, the team had taken the rest of the day off.

"And that's why we're watching the celebration below," explained Geoff, pointing down to the scene on the bank of the lake where Wayne and his team were gathered. "The team's celebrating an accomplishment and the swim provides a good excuse and a lot of good public relations for the project."

"Wow! There he goes!" someone burst out as Chris dove into the water.

Danny shook his head and shivered involuntarily. Then, "I wonder if John Picard can swim?" he asked Geoff thoughtfully. They both broke down laughing.

[T]he most effective way of utilizing human energy is through an orga-nized rivalry, which by specialization and social control is, at the same time, organized co-operation.

   Charles Horton Cooley in Human Nature and the Social Order

Chapter 15

The Celebration

There's no point in success if you don't let it go to your head. That's what it's for.

> John Otway, British rock musician

A T NINE A.M., the bright spring day had just gotten off to a good start when Geoff walked into John's office. "John, the Systems Group is having a short meeting in a few minutes," he announced. "and I thought you might want to go with me."

"I don't know anything about systems," John answered. "What kind of meeting?"

"Actually, it's a small celebration. The group reached their goal of a half million dollars in net savings for the project." Geoff smiled as he explained, "Bobby Taylor read about a new process they're using in our Santiago Office and sent one of his techies down to have a look. It took some work but we were able to reconfigure our system and the new system not only cost less, but will save our client about $10,000 a year in operating costs. That savings pushed us over the top and actually was about half of the systems group's goal."

"I knew Bobby was going down to Chile but I didn't know why," John thought out loud. "Did you know the potential when you authorized the trip?"

"I didn't actually authorize the trip," Geoff said as they headed toward the meeting room. "You remember the allocation I asked for a couple of months ago? The one to investigate technological breakthroughs that might help the project? I set up a small team representing each of the technical aspects of the project and gave them the budget. They allocated the trip. This trip alone will leverage our investment at about ten to one. Not bad, given the high risk potential. I was actually only hoping to break even."

"Sounds like it turned out even better than you hoped." John commented.

Geoff just smiled as he thought, *What a crazy way to run a project! You walk into the project manager's office without the slightest warning and say 'let's go to a meeting.' The next thing you know you're* *explaining that you didn't authorize a trip that on most projects would require the project manager's signature—no reaction. You say you turned over $25,000 to a team and said "find me a breakthrough that will double that investment" and you get a 'Sounds like it turned out better than you hoped." If I had lost it all, the response would have probably been 'Sounds like it didn't go as well as you had hoped." I always wanted the decision-making authority I've got on this project but I never understood the impact it would have on my decision-making process. Now I make the decision but I am also responsible and just as I am learning to handle that, John starts encouraging me to share it. To empower others with both the authority and the responsibility.*

Geoff realized that he and John had walked the length of the hall while he was thinking. He paused at the door. "This small celebration," he told John, "is a result of my learning to empower others, which was a direct result of your empowering the entire project team. The results are speaking for themselves."

Geoff and John walked in the conference room as the last of the Systems Team arrived. Coffee and donuts were on the table and discussion was focused more on the Atlanta Braves than on work. John and Geoff talked with some familiar members of the team and added their thoughts to the chances of finding a team that could beat the Braves this year.

Desi Moore, the Systems Team leader, went to the front of the room and people started finding seats around the table. Desi thanked John and Geoff for coming to their celebration and briefly went over the challenges the team had faced a couple of months before. She described how Bobby Taylor and a small team had discovered the opportunity in Chile and the agonizing process the team had gone through in deciding to allocate so much of their budget to that one opportunity.

Desi then called on Geoff to say a few words. Geoff reached under the table and pulled out a large paper bag, which he carried to the front of the room while people offered all kinds of wild guesses what could be in it. Just as Geoff was finishing a few jokes, Hal Campbell walked into the room.

"Okay, people." Geoff said loudly, for Hal's benefit. "Explain to me again how you figured out a way to save our client another two million dollars?" Hal laughed as he shook hands with Geoff and turned to find a seat. "Remember that line," Geoff said, turning back to the team. "You never know when a client is going to walk into your meeting!"

Geoff then reached into the bag and pulled out a large scroll. "Bobby Taylor, would you come to the front of the room, please," he said in an exaggerated voice of authority. "Desi and I want to present you and your team with a proclamation that reflects the honor and prestige your team has brought forth upon this project ..."

Geoff and Desi read the document they had spent two lunch hours developing. They'd included humorous tidbits about everyone on the team and the team enjoyed hearing it read almost as much as Desi and Geoff enjoyed developing it.

Then Geoff invited John and Hal to join him at the front of the room. Together, with great ceremony, they gave every member of the team a T-shirt with the project logo and *THE WORLD'S GREATEST SYSTEMS TEAM* emblazoned on the front.

Hal expressed his personal appreciation and acknowledged the team's accomplishments in few words. He told them that a member of his team had labeled the project "The World's Greatest Project" several weeks ago in jest when asked what project he was working on. The name stuck because it was humorous, but also reflected what most of the team really felt. So people at Hal's company had started referring to the project as the WGP. Hal then handed out to all the team members something that looked like a business card, personalized with the project logo and person's name embossed in gold. Across the top it read: *MEMBER OF THE WGP.*

"A Remarkable Silence"

John and Hal were heading back to their seats when Bobby Taylor stood up. "Just a minute, we have something for you, too. The Systems Team has noticed a remarkable silence on this project. Several comments we usually hear were missing. So, to make all our lives more comfortable, we developed a list of comments usually heard around a project that should worry a project manager."

Bobby started and then each member of the team offered their suggestion of the statement that should most worry a project manager. John borrowed a pad and took notes during the roundtable presentation as each quote drew laughs and boos. It was valuable information and a lot of fun, too. John was surprised to find, as they left the room, that the entire celebration had lasted less than thirty minutes.

As they walked together towards their offices, Geoff remarked to John, "I think that rates high on the celebration of successes."

119

"It's a good team and they did a good job," John acknowledged.

"I mean it was a good *celebration*," Geoff clarified. "Remember Ken's guidelines for celebrating success? I think that celebration hit every single suggestion Ken provided."

"I remember," John said as they entered Geoff's office. "A good overall approach is to focus on what you are truly trying to accomplish with the celebration."

"Let's compare it to Ken's list," Geoff said as he searched the top of his desk. Very quickly he found what he was looking for and started going down his list.

1. We focused on the achievement and why it was valuable.
2. We were specific in our thanks.
3. The celebration took place within a week of the accomplishment.
4. A senior project manager attended and spoke.
5. A senior client project manager attended and spoke.
6. The celebration took place in the work area.
7. We provided food.

"Looks like we covered all the bases," Geoff said proudly. "Even the donuts were good."

"You're right, Geoff. The celebration met all of Ken's criteria. But how do you feel that it went?" John asked.

Geoff thought for a minute. He had just told John the celebration had met all the criteria for success and yet he was still asking if he thought it was successful ...?

John was aware of Geoff's discomfort and quickly made him more at ease. "Geoff, Ken's formulas are great for focusing your activities and understanding what you are trying to accomplish but you must balance that against your own experience and gut feel. You're very talented at reading people. Use that talent to help you manage your project. Not only was the celebration done the right way," John continued. "but it *felt* right. People were supporting each other, they were at ease and confident, and they were having fun. And you helped make that happen. Good job."

John met Geoff's eyes for a minute and then started down the hall toward his own office, whistling.

Geoff sat down at his desk and started to pick up the telephone but stopped. He was thinking about John's remarks. *Analyze the data but trust your gut.* It was a message of balance, the kind of message John was continually giving Geoff these days. John very seldom provided suggestions on management issues, Geoff now recognized. He was helping Geoff become a leader and the advice was much more subtle and personal. Geoff stared at the telephone for a minute enjoying this realization, then dialed the number. It was time to address the next issue on his list.

JOHN WAS A LITTLE SURPRISED that the cards had been ready. Hal had told him about the idea—although not about the upcoming celebration—during their trip to Nashville the week before.

The Nashville trip had been the second stage of a little management project of their own. The previous month, they had flown to Nashville to talk with the owners of one of their suppliers who was falling behind in deliveries critical to the project schedule. It was a family-owned business known for quality work. When pressured about the schedule by the procurement team, they kept referring back to their reputation for quality. After lengthy discussions with no resolution of the problem, the project management team decided that a trip from John and Hal might make a difference. After all, every day they advanced this vendor was a day for the project.

John and Hal had taken photographs of the project and copies of the project schedule to a meeting with the company president and his son. During the morning, Hal had presented an overview of the project and how the vendor's deliveries fit into the project. He'd showed how they had developed several alternative schedules and how the overtime schedule could only make a small difference. He made it obvious that the vendor was critical to the project's schedule. Finally, Hal asked what the project could do to help the vendor.

That afternoon, the vendor reviewed their work plan and together they identified three areas that were preventing the acceleration of the schedule. Two were caused by deliveries from the vendor's suppliers. Hal and John made a few phone calls and, by the end of the day, they had new commitments to help the vendor make the schedule.

The last problem was their production schedule. The current production line could not meet the project schedule. After a good deal of discussion, John had offered to send a team to help set up a temporary second line. If each of the three shifts on the permanent line worked an additional two hours on the temporary line for four weeks, then the schedule could be met. Hal offered to pay the overtime premium and the cost of John's team to help set up the line. The cost of the line would be more than reimbursed by the schedule bonus the vendor would receive. By the end of the day they'd had a plan that everyone agreed would be successful.

"Your order was shipped last week. However,
according to our shipping records,
last week doesn't begin until next Thursday."

Then, just last week, John and Hal had gone back to Nashville to review the progress. They walked around the shop floor and gave each worker a baseball hat with the project logo and personally thanked them for helping make the project a success. That had never happened before; you could see the positive reaction on the faces of the workers. That night they took the company president and his son to a pleasant dinner. The vendor was now performing ahead of schedule and everybody's confidence was high.

On the plane on the way home, Hal had suggested the business card idea. He had seen something like it before and thought it was great. He'd wanted to give the team members something personal and project-related and thought a "business" card could do both. What surprised John was that Hal had managed to get personalized cards to give out in less than a week.

But that's a project manager for you, he thought with a smile.

John's Notes

Statements that should cause a project manager concern:

We have so many goals we are bound to achieve some of them...

I don't like this system but it is the company's system for tracking ....

We are having so many meetings I can't get my work done ...

Our success is dependent on how hard we work ...

Don't worry about me, you get your part done and turn it over to me and I will finish the project on time ...

We will have to work eighty hours a week and weekends to finish the project on time ...

Why doesn't anybody tell me anything around here ...

Not another team building session!

What does he want, I worked all night on this!

I hear we were awarded the Los Condes Project, can I get an early release?

Why are we celebrating?

You can't trust these numbers, they are trying to protect themselves ...

Be prepared to defend that idea in the staff meeting ...

Innovative ideas will only be accepted on the green idea submission form 32A, with appropriate approval. Submit form in triplicate before 3:00 on Thursdays ....

That can't be true, we tried that on the last project and it didn't work ...

This project is no fun.

Chapter 16

Tapping into Discretionary Effort

Ideas are refined and multiplied in the commerce of minds.
Gaston Bachelard in The Poetics of Reverie

LATE WEDNESDAY AFTERNOON, near quitting time, the project management team gathered in the conference room for a brainstorming session. Jane Roberts had asked John to make a presentation on motivation to the entire division. Apparently Ken had told her that John's project was doing an extraordinary job of tapping into discretionary effort. Now she expected John to make a formal presentation on how the project had tapped into this effort, and he, quite honestly, wasn't sure. He had asked his team to put their heads together to develop thoughts that he could use in his presentation.

After some opening discussion, John summarized what the team thought Ken meant by "discretionary effort."

"There's a certain level of effort that a person cannot go below, at least not for long, without getting fired. That level of effort forms the baseline. Any effort above that baseline is given because people *want* to give it. Therefore, that effort, if we could measure it, could be called 'discretionary.' Almost everybody gives some effort above the baseline, and some people give a great deal more than others. On some projects, everybody on the project gives more. The question is, why?

"Let's put some structure into developing our thoughts," John suggested. "We'll go around the table, giving our thoughts, and I'll record them on the flip chart. Let's try that for awhile and see if we get anywhere. Andre, can you start us off?"

Andre: "Our focus on this project has NOT been on people working harder, but on working smarter. We look at results. All our recognition has centered around accomplishing *goals*. We only look at *activities* when we're looking for better ways to improve our work process. We encourage innovation. Maybe that discretionary effort was directed toward creative activities that produced a better product with less effort."

124

John made short, precise notes on the flip chart as Andre spoke. Then Andre turned to Danny, on his right, indicating that it was his turn.

Danny: "Building on your thought, Andre, I remember how hard it was for me to walk the project floor and see people talking and NOT jump someone's case. John pulled me back several times, reminding me that we were getting great results. Our focus should never be on the hour-to-hour activities of the project team, but on providing feedback about how they're doing toward meeting goals."

Lucy: "I think people enjoyed giving that effort because they were 'stakeholders.' They bought into the project vision and understood what we were trying to achieve. Everybody understood how they contributed to project success. It took a lot of work, sharing all kinds of information and charts, but people needed that information in order to know how they were contributing to success."

Geoff: "Something special. We created a special project from the beginning. Something people wanted to join. If you're doing something special and see something meaningful coming out of it, you give more because you get more out of it. Celebrations, visits from top management and letters from the client, all reinforce this feeling of specialness."

John wrote as fast as he could, trying to capture the ideas. They had already gone around the table once and were waiting for John to catch up and share his own ideas. But John simply turned around and gave Andre a slight nod.

Andre knew exactly what that nod meant. In six short months, the team had learned to talk in shorthand and communicate without talking. *We've become more efficient in our communications, and I wonder if that has impacted our performance?* he thought, but he decided to share a more important topic.

Andre: "We're having fun. Work is easier when you're having fun, and if work is easier, you can give a lot more without getting tired."

Danny: "We empowered people to achieve their goals. Nobody wasted effort waiting on someone else to do their job first. Everybody was a partner and a problem solver. If they needed information, they went after it and didn't wait for the formal distribution of a report with the information."

Lucy: "I've been thinking about the impact of money on this issue. Everybody knows we're going to get bonuses based on the project saving money and being completed on time, but we on the project don't determine salaries. We have input, but the department heads make the money call. So the bonuses themselves, while nice, are not intrinsic motivators. I think the bonuses mean more as *symbols* of our roles as stakeholders; because people are part of the success, they share in the success. The little things give the same message: donuts and coffee on special mornings, celebrations, special lunches, all say *we are interested in you, and we want you to know it.*"

Geoff: "Trust. People on this project trusted the management team. We earned that trust and never abused it. We didn't blow smoke. We communicated our trust by the things we communicated and the way we communicated. People didn't have to spend useless energy watching their backs or playing politics. I know we had some politics going on, of course, but the project as a whole was focused on goals, directed toward milestones, and was people-oriented."

Andre: "We listened and showed respect. When Geoff says we were people-oriented, I ask myself, how did the team know that? We did show respect and listened to ideas as well as concerns. I'll never forget the heads nodding around the room when John told Ken to include families in celebrations whenever possible. I think that meant something to everybody, and in turn, people cared about the success of the project."

Danny: "We squashed the NIH—the 'Not Invented Here' syndrome will kill a company this size because good ideas that can help increase performance are ignored because we didn't think of them ourselves. I remember John telling Andre to go to the Houston office, steal every good idea he could from them, and then gave us one month to improve on their ideas. But then he took our new and improved idea and gave the credit to Houston. We got good ideas; people improved them and felt ownership, and Houston got to feel part of the success because we were using their ideas."

Lucy: "I'm still thinking about recognition. We recognized excellence—and even inspired managers on other projects to do the same. Remember the Lester Challenge? During the entire two hour celebration, not a single manager took the stage. The quality team set the goal, tracked the progress, arranged the celebration, and managed the entire effort without management's direct involvement. That's empowerment! I think people realized that the managers were there to be supportive, but that it was *their* success and they were getting the recognition. Sometimes, people need for others to see and recognize their success for them to feel successful."

Geoff: "Expectations. We set a tone and developed an expectation at the beginning of the project that we required the best. I remember a letter I wrote to the client early on. John saw it, took a red pen and bled all over it! I was a little sloppy with that letter. His message was very clear: we do better work than that on this project. It was an expectation, not chastisement. If expectations are not high, then where's the challenge? High but reachable expectations set the tone and when people respond, goals are achieved and projects are successful."

Lucy: "I think another motivator was feedback. We let every team and person know how they were doing against goals, and when something slipped, we didn't look for blame, we developed a recovery plan. The message was that we meet all goals and exceed most."

Danny: "Our quality teams impacted motivation in two ways: One, the teams actually solved problems that impacted our goals and, two, the problem solvers helped make the solution work because it was *their* solution."

John stopped writing and sat down at the table, partly because he had writer's cramp, but also because he was thinking about something Ken had talked about not long ago. John shared with the team his thoughts about "official goals," those goals declared by management, and "operative goals," the goals that are actually reinforced.

"A project will always get in trouble when management's *official* goals are displaced by different *operative* goals—and still worse is when following the rules or adherence to policy becomes the goal in itself."

Time to quit and go home, John noted, glancing at his watch. It was hard to believe that people were now getting their work done, goals were being met, and making it home without the long hours that had been the norm at the start of the project. He rolled up the flip chart paper and whistled a tune as he headed to his office to draw up an outline. He'd known that the brainpower of this team would produce more thoughts than he could ever cover in a divisional meeting, and as usual, they hadn't disappointed him.

John's Notes

Focus on Goals, not Performance

Make People Shareholders

Drive Innovation

Create a Feeling of Something Special

Set Clear Expectations

Empower People

Give Good Feedback

Recognize People's Successes

Use Quality Teams

Create a Project Environment of Trust

Demonstrate Your Respect for People—Listen!

Squash "NIH"

Make Operative and Official Goals the Same

Encourage FUN!

Chapter 17

In the Crayon Room: the Creative Process

Whatever creativity is, it is in part a solution to a problem.

Brian Aldiss in Apéritif

L UCY HAD ASKED Danny, Geoff and Andre to convene in the small conference room, the one they called "the crayon room," for a lunch meeting. The project had a "war room," a large conference room with the walls covered with project measurements, and two smaller conference rooms for small team meetings.

Geoff had given the crayon room its name at the beginning of the project when Andre was struggling to get his project measurements completed and displayed. After two weeks of software, hardware, network and printer problems John had finally told him, "Let's get our measurements on the wall even if you have to use crayons!" Andre and his team worked late that night and the next morning all the key project measurements were on the wall, in crayon. That afternoon John went around to everybody on Andre's team and gave each of them a giant box of new crayons. Although measurements from the monthly report were now reproduced by computer and displayed on the client's progress board, some of the measurements in the war room and small conference rooms, which were easily made, hand-drawn charts, were still done in crayon. Members of Andre's team who had been on the project from the beginning proudly displayed their boxes of crayons on their desks.

The crayon room was the perfect place for the task Lucy had planned; small, almost cozy, it created a sense of informality and creativity.

"John asked us to get together to capture the lessons we learned on this project before we start getting too focused on planning our next assignment," Lucy began. "I thought we would just brainstorm ideas, maybe a list of quotes, or some do's and don'ts. John said he wasn't looking for a formal report, just a deliverable that we can take with us and build on during our next project."

129

Lucy looked around to gauge the reaction, and Andre picked up the ball. "Why don't we just go around the room and throw out ideas and I'll capture them on the whiteboard."

"The first one is easy," Geoff started the process. "The five most important roles of project managers are to plan, coordinate, communicate, communicate and communicate."

"So you think communication is important?" Danny laughed, as Andre wrote on the board:

Communicate

"I've changed my perspective on my role on this project," Geoff answered. "I used to be the biggest complainer that I couldn't get my job done because of all the meetings, e-mails, memos, and phone calls. Then it occurred to me that those meetings, conferences, calls and memos *were* my job. My role is to plan, coordinate and communicate and I can't do that sitting in my office with the door closed. I know I need quiet time to get my thoughts together—time to focus on what's *important*, not just what's *urgent*. Some of my most creative thinking happens when I'm alone picturing a project event. But without the personal contact with all the project teams, I wouldn't be able to do my job. One of my greatest personal improvements on this project has been increasing my capacity to communicate my message."

"How would you capture that concept in a short statement that I can write on the board?" Andre asked.

"*Sending* a message does NOT equal *communicating* a message." Lucy offered.

"That's not exactly it, Lucy." Geoff responded. "That's a good thought, though. I learned that some people understand the message better if it is written, while others want to hear it. Everybody seems to receive messages differently. I'm not talking about how messages often get mixed up. We did a good job of communicating messages in many different ways: newsletters, charts on the wall, meetings—even our celebrations were a communication opportunity.

"What I mean is I cannot manage from my office. I need to hear what people are thinking, see what people are doing and make sure everyone understands the needs of the project."

"How about 'You can't manage a project from an office,'" Lucy suggested.

"That's great, Lucy," Andre said as he wrote. "All we need is a short statement that helps us capture the lessons we learned on the project. Something that will jog our memory when we read it next."

"Starting today, everyone in this office will share the same doughnut and coffee. It's part of our new emphasis on teamwork."

The salads arrived. After a year on the project, Lucy knew everybody's preferences and had ordered salads and drinks for the team. Lunch meetings were common on the project, although reserved for lighter topics. After a few minutes of passing out the food and taking the first few bites, the team was ready to resume their conversation.

"Yes, but it's more than that. Remember Ken's formula for communications?" Geoff asked. "That communications was a function of the difficulty of the communication times the clarity of the message times the trust between the communicators."

"Ken only provided formulas for you techies, Geoff," Andre kidded as he wrote:

Communications = (Difficulty x Clarity x Trust)

"Okay, what else," Lucy asked, moving the team on to a new topic. Communication was always the first topic on any management improvement list, but the dimensions of communications were so complex the team could eat up the entire lunch meeting discussing communication.

"I've got one," Danny volunteered. "Nothing impacts a project as much as inefficient meetings. I have learned more about the types of meetings, how to facilitate a meeting, when and where to have meetings on this project than I think I will ever remember."

"Building on that thought," Lucy suggested, "isn't it true that every project seems to have the same number of meetings? You have to either spend time in *planning meetings* or you will spend time in *problem solving meetings*."

"Boy, is that true!" Danny responded. "On the Mexico Project we spent so much time fixing problems that we never had time to plan. The lack of planning caused problems that took time away from planning that caused problems that ... it was a downward spiral that was very difficult to break."

Geoff cleared the salad dishes as Andre recorded the last suggestions. The team sat thinking for a while before Danny suggested another quote. "If the message is negative, the results will be negative."

"Danny, you're still focused on the Mexico Project," Geoff reminded him. "We're supposed to be talking about the lessons learned on *our* project."

"Okay," Danny revised his quote. "If the message is positive, the results will be positive."

Everyone smiled as Lucy nodded, "That's more like it."

Andre recorded Danny's suggestion and sat down. The team seemed contemplative. The expressions on people's faces suggested some deep thinking to Andre. This team had developed a comfort with short periods of silence.

"I learned a lot about building trust, too," Geoff offered quietly after a while.

Trust

"Trust was a key element of our success," Danny agreed. "I know I've had more open and honest communication on this project than any other project in my career—maybe more than any activity in my life. I'm not sure how it developed, but I remember I made a huge mistake on the cost forecast and my immediate response was to bring it up to the team and ask for your help. In the past, I would have worked hard to fix the problem before you found out, so that by the time you found out, I could say it was all fixed. But the best response to any problem on this project was an open discussion with the team.

"Of course, trust means something different on a project—maybe in business relationships generally. My teammates on the Mexico Project were my friends—just as you guys are. I trusted them personally, but the difference here, on this project, is in how that personal trust is translated into the way we communicate and deal with each other on a day by day basis," Danny said thoughtfully.

"I'm not saying this well, let me try it again," he continued after a pause. "I developed a trust in this team that enabled me to admit when I needed help. You, my team, were a source of strength. When I was down you gave me energy. And just as important, I was a contributor. Because you trusted me, I was a helper as well. Together we build on our strengths. We were greater than the sum total of the individuals.

"I don't mean to get all mushy or anything," Danny quickly added, a little embarrassed. "But the difference between this project and the Mexico Project was the difference between enjoying work and having to work for a living. The difference was the relationship I have with the team and that was built on trust—not just in people but in our mutual commitment to the project goals."

Lucy asked him, "How do you think we built that trust?"

"I'm not sure," Danny replied. "We have an affection for each other built on just knowing each other personally. On projects, people are thrown together for one or two years and the risk in a relationship is smaller. Again, on the Mexico Project, I remember a friend saying that the project would only last two years and he could take anything for two years. That was his way of dealing with the stuff going on around him. In that environment there was no need to resolve small conflicts; you just tolerated the discomfort until it was over. But I don't see how that builds trust."

"Two thoughts occur to me," Andre jumped in. "At church I have long-term relationships with people. Those friendships will be a significant part of my life for a long time. I can build these relationships over time. If I have a disagreement with someone, I have plenty of time to work through it. I have no sense of urgency. I am a little careful and take time in developing those relationships. Trust develops slowly.

"But on a project, I feel the need to build ties quickly. We have work to do and need to work together and get on with it. That sense of urgency and the understanding that a mistake only has short-term consequences probably encourages us to develop relationships more quickly."

"Maybe people who work on projects develop special skills that allow them to develop the relationships they need to work in a project environment," Lucy suggested.

"Well, I just think John put the right team together," Geoff said. "I knew everybody on the team by reputation and everybody had the reputation of being hardworking, professionally competent and honest. Those are the personal characteristics I look for in someone if I am going to trust them."

"Except the Mexico Project team also had those characteristics," Danny pointed out. "But I think trust disappeared when the project manager did things like altering meeting notes just a little to make it look like a small problem had resulted from the client's delay in a decision, rather than from our inability to produce the work. Although that was a smart management move and it positioned us better if we ever got in legal hassles with the client, we all then knew the rules to go by on that project: Decisions and behaviors were based on the maximum advantage to the company—and probably to the project manager."

"Actually, that might have provided a higher degree of trust," Geoff countered. "You could 'trust' the project manager's behavior. You could trust he would work in self-interest and therefore you could predict and prepare for his response. That's a simple and workable definition of trust."

"Maybe," Danny said. "But you couldn't trust the project data. If numbers and comments are manipulated, even slightly, to make the project look a certain way, you lose confidence in your numbers and that's a poor situation for making informed decisions."

"Didn't your client pick up on that?" asked Lucy.

"Again, we're not talking about major issues here," Danny said strongly. "I don't think of him as dishonest. He just interpreted the data in a way that made him and the project look better."

"And your client didn't know that? Lucy asked again.

"He knew," Danny replied softly. "I think that's why things between them were always a little strained. People labeled it a personality conflict, but I think those little manipulations caused a breach in trust and problems for the project."

"How would you rate John?" Geoff asked.

"I know John's values. His behavior is consistent with those values," Danny answered. "He's always encouraged us to be open and honest with Hal and his team. There were at least a dozen times when we could have interpreted data just a little differently, but John's response was so strong, you knew his expectations immediately. We were partners with this client and we had better be honest."

"I think that's part of why we developed trust so quickly on the project," Lucy interjected. "John doesn't tolerate dishonesty. I can think of nothing that would get you removed from John's project faster than dishonesty. He doesn't tolerate even the smallest breach. He walks the talk—and he talks loudly!"

"If trust on a team comes from the values, expectations and behavior of the leader, John sure instilled trust in this team," Andre agreed.

"I think John's example was important, but he did some concrete things that helped, too," Geoff said. "We had the retreat to kick off the project. Remember the little games Ken led us through to get to know each other? Sometimes they were silly and sometimes I was very uncomfortable with the honest talk about myself. But when we left, I knew that Andre loved horses, Danny understood life through sports analogies, and," Geoff smiled at Lucy "Lucy would be a source of strength for me. You really don't have to be friends to trust and work together but, it makes the project easier and more enjoyable."

"That kind of trust is personal," Andre added. "It goes beyond our project. I have developed an affection and respect for each of you, as well as for John. That's because I have come to know, respect and trust you. I trust you like I do my own family."

"I agree with Andre," Lucy said. "Much of the trust we share is based on mutual respect—but as a lesson learned, we can't put something like that down."

"No, but we can say something basic like 'develop mutual respect' and we will all know what we mean." Geoff got up and went to the whiteboard. The meeting transitioned into a more structured discussion and, as had often happened on the project, the meeting's leadership transitioned to a member with a more structured style. He wrote:

Official vs. Operative rules

As Geoff wrote, Andre said, "We were always consistent. We never stated a project rule and then operated as if that rule didn't exist. If we said something, you could take it to the bank. Our official rules, the rules we set, and the operative rules, the rules we reinforced, were always the same."

"What else?" Geoff asked the group.

"Maintain respect," Danny said. "The leadership team has always shown public respect for each other. For example," he continued, suppressing a grin, "I would never point out in any meeting outside this group that you just took over Lucy's meeting by going to the whiteboard."

Geoff stopped writing and turned, embarrassed, looking first at Danny and then at Lucy.

"Don't even respond to that, Geoff," Lucy said lightly. "We learned a long time ago to work as a team where leadership is always shared and shifts, depending on the needs of the group and who has the most energy. But, outside his attempt to be humorous," Lucy said as she made a little face at Danny, "he has a good point. We have always honored each other's self-respect."

"But don't we do that on every project?" Andre asked. "I mean, that's not unique to John's project."

"You're right, Andre," Danny answered. "But some small things can make a big difference. At the start of the Mexico Project, we had some difficulty getting our act together around requesting checks for payment. Nobody was following policy because our systems weren't set yet. Our client discovered some of the problems and went looking for what was going wrong. He focused on the administrative manager and gave her a pretty hard time. Not a single member of the project leadership team stood up in her defense. I'm embarrassed that I, too, sat in silence, hoping I wouldn't be next. That was a miserable experience and it was one of those experiences that destroyed the trust on that project. I hope I'm never tested like that again."

"But you *have* been tested, Danny," Lucy reminded him. "Remember when Hal was jumping all over me for not paying vendors at the beginning of the project? You came back quickly that you had taken more time than allocated to review their invoices before you gave them to me. You looked Hal in the face and said that you would set up a team to flow-diagram the work process. We improved the process and never missed another scheduled payment."

"But that was different, Lucy," Danny replied. "I remember that. I'm not sure why, but it wasn't hard to speak up and admit that I was having a problem. I knew we would address and solve it as a team."

"We're running out of time," Geoff said, still standing at the whiteboard.

"I know," Lucy said. "Let's try to capture a few more points to write down."

"Some of the old rules of project management don't hold water," Andre suggested. As Geoff wrote:

The Old Rules Don't Always Apply

Andre continued, "Like the three-legged stool model that has been around project management for years."

"I remember being taught that model in graduate school," Lucy responded with energy. "That the three legs of project management: cost, schedule, and quality, were always in balance. That you can improve one or maybe two but always at the cost of the third. I remember, on my last project, telling our client we could finish the project faster but it would cost more money or else he would have to lower the specs. I was following that rule of project management. You couldn't have your cake and eat it too. But on this project, we significantly impacted all three! The old rules don't always apply and they surely didn't apply to our project."

"I remember Hal asking us to shorten the project schedule by two weeks so they could take advantage of some tax laws," Andre said, by way of example. "We set up a team to determine the cost of reducing the project schedule by two weeks. The team developed a creative approach that both met Hal's schedule needs and improved the quality of the project's deliverables. Hal named the team the Dream Team after they reported the total project cost would actually decrease. That was the first example where we proved the old rule wrong and it set up a supportive atmosphere where innovative solutions were encouraged."

"How about this old rule," Geoff suggested. "'If I work harder I will get more done.' One thing I've learned is the law of diminishing returns does not have a stopping point. At some point you can work so hard, for so long you start undoing past progress." Geoff grinned broadly as he added, "Einstein said that matter consists mainly of space connected by energy— energy so strong that the release of this energy has a tremendous impact. I'm suggesting that *a project is people connected by mental energy, and when that energy is released the impact is just as powerful.*"

Everyone absorbed Geoff's statement in silence for a moment; then Lucy began to applaud. Danny and Andre joined in until Geoff's face turned red.

"I knew this project was good, but you don't think we've discovered a new application of relativity?" Danny laughed.

"No, but we proved that both Geoff and Einstein are pretty smart," Andre joked.

"Wow, look at the time. Sorry to break up the party, folks," Danny stood and stretched, "but 'Einstein' and I have to go. We're meeting with Hal's team on the new project start-up in fifteen minutes."

"I think we have enough to get started on some deliverables for John," Lucy concluded. "I'll get a draft circulated tomorrow."

Good Leadership Makes the Difference

Falsehood is invariably the child of fear in one form or another.
Aleister Crowley in The Confessions of Aleister Crowley

As she took down the notes from the whiteboard, Lucy thought about the project and the contribution of the various players. Ken, Geoff, Danny, Andre, and even Hal had contributed significantly, but the bottom line was that this had been John's project. The team had built trust based on John's example and expectations. He'd also provided a workshop that gave the team a jumpstart. He had the confidence to bring in a Ken-type person. He'd given Geoff the freedom and support he needed to develop his management skills. "We can talk all we want to about how we developed as a team," Lucy thought, "but it was the gentle hand of John—and sometimes the not-so-gentle-hand—that created the foundation for the team."

Lucy remembered a conversation she'd had with Ken, in which she had given Ken the credit for the success of the project. "You were the linchpin of the project," she'd told Ken. "You brought in the ideas, the concepts and the support for the team to develop."

But Ken had quickly straightened her out.

This had been Ken's sixth project as a quality facilitator. The first four of those projects had been hugely successful; so successful that Ken began to get a reputation as the creator of successful projects. Then came the fifth project: the Snowbird Project.

Not much was known in the company about the Snowbird Project. Lucy didn't know anyone except Ken who'd been involved in it, and he seldom spoke about it. Except on this occasion, when he felt Lucy was giving him too much credit for the current project's success.

It was then that Ken and Lucy had a lengthy, private lunch. Ken had explained that the Snowbird Project had been fast-track. A big bonus for finishing the project early had driven the team to set highly aggressive targets. Although those targets were not any higher than John's project, the Snowbird Project had no plans for reaching them, other than just "work hard."

138

The difference, as Ken explained at lunch, was that the Snowbird Project had no overall project direction. Planning had been done at the working level of the project. Each functional manager was responsible for developing a plan and integrating that plan with all the other functions of the project. They never developed a "Snowbird Team." The project maximized the *functions* of the project at the cost of the *whole*. And the whole therefore became less than the sum of its parts!

Although Ken had understood what was happening, he was unable to influence the team. Lucy had found this hard to believe. Ken came with credibility and always provided recommendations that made sense and a process for implementing his suggestions. But on the Snowbird Project, the project manager apparently did not believe that his role was to manage the team; instead, he was focused on the business and profitability of the project, and expected the functional managers to execute the project.

During their lunch, Lucy learned that Ken carried a deep regret about the outcome of the Snowbird Project. But Ken had learned a lot from the project and he continued to emphasize the critical role of a project manager in pulling it all together.

"The bottom line is clear," Ken had told Lucy. "John created the environment of trust and the expectation for excellence. John facilitated the development of a team with our client. He set the stage for innovation and reinforced supporting behaviors. He created a project where morale was high, work was focused, trust was universal and success was expected."

Lucy had gotten Ken to admit that he'd added a great deal in each of the areas, providing strong counsel and honest feedback, but Ken stuck by his point and finally, she'd had to agree with him: John was the creator and Ken's role was supportive.

Now, as she finished documenting the results of their "lessons learned" brainstorming session, Lucy realized that this division of roles had worked very well indeed.

Every violation of truth is not only a sort of suicide in the liar, but is a stab at the health of human society.

Ralph Waldo Emerson in Essays

Lucy's List:

"Lessons Learned"

Communicate

"Sending a message doesn't equal communicating a message."
"You can't manage a project from an office"
"Communications = Difficulty x Clarity x Trust"
"Nothing impacts a project more than inefficient meetings."
"You either spend time in planning meetings, or later you will spend time in problem solving meetings."

Trust

"Be totally honest."
"Develop mutual respect."

Make Official and Operation Rules Consistent

"Don't state a rule and then operate as if it doesn't exist."

The Old Rules Don't Always Apply

"Cost, schedule and quality are not always a tradeoff—you can have your cake and eat it too!"
"$P = HE^n$. A Project is Human beings connected by Energy, raised to the *nth* power by trust, shared goals, and good leadership."

Good Leadership Makes the Difference.

Chapter 18

Managing Complexity

*Everything is complicated; if that were not so, life and poetry and every-
thing else would be a bore.*

Wallace Stevens in Letters of Wallace Stevens

KEN HAD JUST arrived and turned on his computer to check his
e-mail when Geoff came in.

"Ken, you got a minute?" Geoff asked. "Jane Roberts has asked
me to develop some way for the division to measure the complexity on a
project. She has this perception that we're not performing as well on
complex projects and we need to understand how complexity impacts
our approach to project management. If complexity is a real factor, then
we'll probably need to develop special tools and techniques to support
what she called *high-complexity projects.*"

"That sounds like a time-consuming task," answered Ken. "I
thought your role on the project took up enough of your time to keep
you out of trouble."

"Yeah, well—I talked with John and he's very supportive. It's a
short-term assignment, but one that may mean a lot on my future
assignments." He made an expression that meant, *and you know what
that means!*

"Oh, I see. Well, I don't have anything until the project staff
meeting at ten o'clock," Ken suggested.

"I did my preparation for the staff meeting last night so I could
have some free time this morning," Geoff said. "So if you have the time,
I would like to just do some free-thinking with you before the project
meeting."

"Sure," Ken agreed. "Let's get a cup of coffee and get started."

Ken knew that Ms. Roberts gave "portfolio assignments" to
selected managers to help prepare them for future assignments. This
task probably meant that Geoff would be managing a complex project
on his next assignment. These portfolio assignments also provided the
division with some innovative thinking, always driving the level of
performance and challenging established ways of doing things.

Geoff also knew that this assignment was important to his career. He would be working directly for Ms. Roberts, which would give her an opportunity to evaluate his reputation for efficiency and innovation. Geoff knew that he not only had to develop a well-thought-out product that would demonstrate an understanding of project complexity, but he also had to develop a product that could impact the way the division evaluated and addressed project complexity.

"How do you want to proceed?" asked Ken.

"I talked with John first and he thinks this is a good assignment for me. Although I still have to get my project work done, John will help me meet my new deadlines. I can do a lot of the research and writing at home but I still need time to talk with people like you. I started yesterday by talking with Danny," Geoff continued. "Danny just came off the project in Mexico and had some interesting experiences. His experience was less than great. Not the model we would want to show our clients. So John suggested I talk with you—that your project experience in Brazil and your people-focus would be valuable."

Ken waited as Geoff gathered his thoughts.

"What made your project in Brazil complex?" Geoff asked after a moment. "Just freewheel it."

"Well, remember, that was over two years ago," answered Ken. "Brazil has changed a lot. This is a country that's opening up to world economic markets. Issues that we needed to deal with are disappearing. Two years ago, inflation was over 100 percent per year, it was hard to get your money out of the country, banks charged you forty dollars for every deposit and every withdrawal, and the government owned everything. All that has changed. Brazil is a much easier place to conduct business now and you can see it in their growth rates."

"Even though your specific issues maybe disappearing," Geoff interjected, "you were successful on a complex project. Tell me why the project was complex and how you managed the complexity."

Ken first described the client. The project had been an investment by two American companies who formed a partnership, found the technical expertise they wanted in an Australian company, and found the local market knowledge they needed with a firm in Brazil. All of these companies came together to form a new business enterprise. A board of directors was named from representatives of each company and a new corporation formed to operate the business and execute the first project.

This new entity contracted with Ken's team to develop and execute its first project. It involved a new technology, so team members came from all over the world. The project manager was from Texas and his technical manager from Alberta, Canada. The procurement manager was from California and the controls manager was from South Africa. The team had so many accents that even though English was the common language, misunderstandings were a daily occurrence.

"The organization must have been a nightmare," observed Geoff. "Was your client's project manager part of the success?"

"Interesting question." Ken pondered. "I believe the client's project manager is always part of your success—but never part of your failure. I don't mean that in a blaming sense. Part of our job is to increase the effectiveness of the client. To translate the business goals of the client into project goals in such a way that our project goals are important to the client's success. If we are tied through mutual goals and the criteria for success is the same for both teams, then you and your client can create one project team.

"That probably oversimplifies our project," Ken continued. "The client's team was located in three different countries. We were concerned from the beginning about our ability to gauge the client's perception of the project. So we developed a monthly client survey with the client's project manager to measure the client team's perception of our performance. We wanted some feedback to tell if we were on track with our focus and performance. I sent a one-page survey to each member of the client's team to complete and return to me. I got these faxes, about ten each month, and I summarized the results for our team to review.

"I kept the individual surveys confidential and just gave a team summary. The results were always looked forward to by our team. We discussed the issues that were brought up and developed a plan to address every single issue. We then discussed our plan with the client until we had a joint approach. Sometimes these discussions were heated, but usually we quickly came to consensus on how we wanted to deal with issues."

"Didn't a monthly survey become a paperwork hassle?" Geoff asked.

"One of the powers of this tool was the intense interest people had in the results," Ken answered. "Many times the client's project manager was surprised by the comments of his own team. The survey became a communication tool for the entire project. This interest on the part of both teams overcame the resistance to 'just another report' syndrome.

"I've had projects where the client's project team gave us a team response rather than individual responses," he went on. "But on a large multilocation project, individual responses seem best."

143

"If this is like the client survey on our project, I can see how it benefits the project," Geoff mused. "On an international project, it would take on an even higher priority. So when a project increases in complexity because of distance between team members, gauging people's perceptions of the project becomes more important and a simple survey can help you gauge these perceptions."

"I'm not sure this adds anything to your complexity task," Ken added, "but I believe the real power of the client survey is the ability to do what John calls a 'system cleanout.' Events on the project, especially on high-pressure or complex projects, create an atmosphere where people sometimes miscommunicate, or we say something a little stronger than we meant to, and these events start building up in people. These rather small events build to create an impression that things are not going well or the system's not working. John says the system gets clogged with minutia and needs cleaning out. The survey acts as a catalyst. If someone has an issue that is bugging them, no matter how small, they can put it on the survey. If they choose not to address the issue, they usually drop it. So you can see why John calls it a cleanout. Without the survey, the buildup continues until either someone explodes at a meeting or—more likely—at the end of the project. Either way the project gets sidetracked."

"Ken, I've been here almost an hour and we've just touched on one aspect of project complexity. Let's refocus on the concept of project complexity. What do you think of when I say *project complexity?*" Geoff asked.

"People issues!" Ken responded. "I think about who will be managing the project and what issues they will focus on. How difficult will it be to communicate? Maybe the right word is *organizational* issues. What will the project organization look like?"

For the next half hour, Ken and Geoff discussed how new technologies create unknowns that add complexity to a project, compared to proven technology which has predictable characteristics. They discussed the size and duration of a project, the environment and location, the amount of support from management, and availability of resources. They discussed project management experience and use of management systems, legal and commercial aspects of projects. Ken shared with him the complexity checklist that he had earlier shared with Chris Lester.[7] By the time the project staff meeting was ready to begin, Geoff had five pages of notes.

---

[7] See Chapter 11.

"This project is extremely important, but it has no budget, no guidelines, no support staff and it's due tomorrow morning. At last, here's your chance to really impress everyone!"

As they walked toward the meeting room Geoff joked, "I guess my next assignment will probably be some mega project with brand-new technology, involving scientists from five countries and no two people who speak the same language."

"...on top of the Andes Mountains," Ken added, "with no communication equipment and bandits raiding your camp every night."

" ... and me without a contract or project charter." Geoff said with a smile. Then he stopped and looked at Ken a little more seriously. "Can you imagine, a project with no contract, no policies or procedures, and limited resources! Just my kind of challenge."

"Yes, Geoff, your kind of project—until you get your first change order." They both laughed as they joined John, who was reviewing the staff meeting agenda.

Use Goals to Focus Your Project

Later that day, Geoff saw Ken getting a cup of coffee and brought up the subject again. "I've been thinking," he said. "What would I *really* do if I got a highly complex project? What would I do differently? Do you know what you did differently on your project in Brazil? Danny seemed to think that the difficulty of complex projects prohibits the kind of success we are experiencing on John's project."

As they walked back toward Geoff's office Ken asked, "What kinds of difficulty did Danny have on the Mexico Project?"

"For example, goals. You know how we focus our project on the goals we need to achieve to be successful. Danny gave an example where his project manager in Mexico called a meeting while the entire management team was in town to develop goals for the next month. Danny's project manager had been in a meeting with John where he'd heard John's 'elevator speech' on monthly goals. So he went back to the project to develop the next month's goals just like we do every month.

"Danny said the team was challenged to identify the three most important goals for the next month and they argued and discussed possible goals for over two hours. Finally, the project manager said, 'Send your thoughts to me by e-mail and I'll determine the list of project goals for the month.

"He decided to use all the suggestions and by the end of the month the project had accomplished eight of the eleven goals they'd developed. The next month the number of goals increased and the percent accomplished decreased. By the third month there were forty-seven goals and the complaints became so loud that the project manager declared success and said there was no need for project goals anymore."

"Wow. Well, the inability to agree on project goals is likely a symptom of the project's complexity," Ken theorized. "I see two issues reflected in that story. First, a team must identify with a common *definition* of project success and they must consistently *communicate* on the development and implementation of the plan to achieve that success. The Mexico Project probably had team members at different locations, maybe some language issues, and my bet is the team was made up of members from different companies."

"Right on all counts," Geoff said, impressed. "And Danny indicated that the team sometimes went weeks without meeting."

"Without that regular contact and working through issues a team becomes misaligned," Ken explained. "Even starting with a good focusing workshop and generating the project vision and key goals, constant communication and discussion are needed."

146

"How did the Brazilian Project keep focused?" Geoff asked.

"The project manager forced communication. The project management team met every other week, no exceptions. We had weekly meetings by telephone conference. Our project scorecard, newsletter, and a constant stream of e-mails kept everyone in the communications loop. People sometimes complained about so many meetings and readings they had to do, but as soon as you didn't include some on your distribution list they started complaining about being cut out of the communications loop! It's always a balance between too much and too little communication, but on a complex project I don't see how there can be too much.

"We sometimes met in meeting rooms at airports. The airport in Lima, for instance, has a nice conference room in one of the airline's lounge areas," Ken explained. "Every other month we'd have a retreat, where we spent three days reviewing the entire project and coming up with innovative solutions to some of our problems and removing barriers from the team. These meetings were always held away from the office, usually at a place conducive friendly conversations, like a ski resort."

Geoff smiled. He knew what Ken was describing. The focusing meeting for John's project had been conducted at a resort in the Smoky Mountains and several other times John had taken the team away for a day or two of meetings. These meetings seemed to occur right about the time the stress level on the project was elevating and beginning to impact performance. Ken wasn't sure how he did it, but John seemed to sense when the team needed some special attention.

"Did you say these meetings were *planned* every two months?" Geoff asked. "This type of meeting isn't planned on our current project yet we seem to be able to judge when one is needed. Why did you build so much structure into your meeting schedule?"

"Two reasons," answered Ken. "Because of distance between team members and speed of the project, it was difficult to gauge the team morale, so regularly scheduled meetings made sense. More importantly, the stress level of complex projects is higher and the regular meetings are needed as stress relievers."

"I don't mean to get you off track," Geoff said as he looked at his watch, "but I need to know more about why complex projects are more stressful."

Ken explained that there were a lot more unknowns on a complex project and therefore much less predictability. If the technology is new, the likelihood of the project working as specified is fairly slim. More time is needed in the start-up phase of a project that is applying new

147

technology. When a project is complicated by crossing international boundaries, there's almost always a slip-up somewhere in transferring money, goods or people. Although these glitches are predictable and the project team plans for them, they still create stress.

Ken used the analogy of a building's fire escape plan. To assure that a fire escape plan will work, most offices have an evacuation drill. Although people know that these drills are going to happen occasionally, when they do happen, they're very disruptive and if they impact a deadline, very stressful.

"Some thoughts are starting to come together," Geoff said. "But about a half hour ago you said you had two problems with Danny's description of the project's difficulty in developing goals. That's how we got into this discussion on communication and predictability. Did we cover your second point?"

"Not really." Ken shook his head. "You quoted Danny as saying the team accomplished eight of the ten goals yet their record got steadily worse."

"That's how Danny described it and you can still see his frustration when he talks about the Mexico Project."

"Well, not achieving goals impacts the team's feeling of commitment," Ken said. "When your teammates are depending on you to provide results, even one slip-up has consequences. On John's project we've met every commitment we've made. We're predictable and dependable and these characteristics help the team look forward, instead of over our shoulders. We don't question if our work this week was wasted because some else didn't get their work done. The entire feeling of predictability gives the team energy."

"What about 'stretch' goals?" Geoff asked. "We only achieve about fifty percent of our stretch goals. Doesn't that impact our predictability and team spirit?"

"The difference between our project monthly goals and our stretch goals is the commitment and potential consequences of failure to achieve a goal," Ken answered. "Stretch goals are, by definition, goals that are not *expected* to be done, but if they *could* be done, they'd accelerate the project. Stretch goals are usually activities scheduled for much later in the project but which can be done today if our tasks for the current month are done.

"Achieving our goals is expected, failure to achieve our goals would indicate something wrong on the project. Achieving our stretch goals is *desired*—but not expected. I don't plan my work around the achievement of stretch goals. But I feel like I should add, accomplishing over fifty percent of our stretch goals is a real reason to celebrate!"

Ken and Geoff went to the conference room to summarize their discussions on the whiteboard there. This allowed them to free-think as they wrote. After about an hour, Geoff looked over the board and said, "I think I can develop a product that will satisfy Ms. Roberts. Thanks again, Ken, for helping me organize my thoughts and for your contribution. I know Ms. Roberts will probably circulate my report, but I'll get you a copy as soon as I get it done."

It had been a good exercise; both Ken and Geoff had gained some insights into project complexity. They had a conceptual framework and a tool to help them better organize a project. By evaluating the complexity of a project, Geoff could now bring together a team with the right skills and develop the organizational structure and approach to deal with complex issues.

For his portfolio assignment, he developed a Project Classification System in which all projects were classified according to their complexity. He also developed a supporting organizational matrix that identified the experience, skills and organizational approaches needed by the various classifications. Geoff was truly excited about what he had accomplished. He felt that his work would probably impact the entire division.

In the meantime, Ken was wondering how much of the learning that took place was a product of Ms. Roberts management style—and what role John had in this exercise. The exercise had energized Geoff at a time when the project was difficult for him. But Geoff had involved all the right players and the team was invested in Geoff's effort. The end product was seen as a success for all.

Geoff's Notes

VARIABLES *OUTSIDE* THE PROJECT TEAM.

Clarity of Objectives - The extent to which project details are specified and unambiguous

Risk - The extent to which project risks are neutralized

Support by Management - The extent of continuous support and interest by management, especially top management

Availability of Resources - The extent of adequate and continuous provision of necessary
resources

Linking Mechanisms - The extent to which procedural and contractual links are clear and
understood

Labor Market/ Industrial Relations Climate - The availability of general and specific
industry labor and the hostility or receptiveness of the industrial relations climate

Technology - The extent in which technical problems are still unresolved

Environment/ Location - The effect of weather, culture, economy, remoteness of project
etc.

Size/Duration - Larger projects take longer, requiring the maintenance of drive and enthusiasm; key Players often get transferred.

Ownership/Sponsorship - Private/public, single/multiple, national/international.

VARIABLES *INSIDE* THE PROJECT

Project Organization Structure - Based on the project goals and work balanced against allocation of resources to accomplish the goals and work. Is the work revolutionary or evolutionary? Routine or non-routine? Expedited schedule?

Project Manager's education, skills, experience and competency

Project Team's education, skills, experience and competency

Systems/Procedures.

Chapter 19

John's Challenge

... we cannot refuse our support to a serious venture which challenges the whole of the personality. If we oppose it, we are trying to suppress what is best in man—his daring and his aspirations. And should we succeed, we have stood in the way of that invaluable experience which might have given meaning to life.

Carl Jung in Collected Works

THE AUDITORIUM FILLED with people decked out in their finest; it was a special night for the company. Each year, the Executive Committee of the Board of Directors celebrated successes and recognized special accomplishments with a first-class banquet. Company executives from all over the world gathered during this week to develop or refine their strategies for the upcoming year. Tonight's gala event would close the week's meetings with an excellent meal and the presentation of awards.

John and Judy Picard ate at the head table, sitting next to Mr. Barbier, the chairman of the board. John felt just a little nervous. Although he'd met and talked with Mr. Barbier several times during his career, they were not on a first-name basis. And, to intensify his nervousness, John was the keynote speaker.

Since the company's business was projects, Mr. Barbier had decided that the keynote speaker should be a project manager; not just any project manager, but someone who exemplified the *new* project manager, the kind who would lead project management into the next century. More and more, projects were becoming a means for corporations to get things done, and the company that made significant improvements in the way projects were managed would dominate the market share. Out of over two thousand company projects that had been worked on during the last year, John's had been chosen as the one that best represented the project of the future.

John's thoughts focused not on Judy's obvious enjoyment of the occasion nor on the courteous conversation of the corporate executives, but on his presentation. For weeks he had prepared for this ten minutes in the spotlight, yet now the talk he'd planned seemed so simple, so much like mere common sense, that he worried how it would be received. Too late now! He'd made the decision two weeks ago to lay it all on the line, and he couldn't back away. He was trying hard not to review his notes one last time as Mr. Barbier headed for the podium. The butterflies began to churn as the chairman finished the preliminary introductions and began talking about John's project.

The applause quieted as Mr. Barbier returned to his seat. John took a deep breath and headed to the podium. He'd learned long ago that 'the butterflies' actually helped as long as you kept them under control. Scanning the room quickly, smiling at some familiar faces in the crowd, he started confidently on the speech he had prepared with both his heart and mind.

"FOR A NUMBER OF YEARS, many of our clients have been implementing various aspects of total quality. But when exploring what aspects of Total Quality Management we should apply to our projects, we need not blindly accept the total quality tools that have been successfully applied by our clients and friends who manage within a manufacturing environment. The special characteristics of projects require special tools and techniques—or at least thoughtful, creative applications of those tools.

"First, let's make sure we agree on what we are talking about. Total Quality Management can be defined as *'the application of tools and techniques to understand, manage and meet customer expectations.'* At first, I was concerned about the way our clients might react when they saw that managing client expectations was part of our job. But when they learn that the biggest part of managing expectations is keeping the client informed on what we plan to do and what to expect, they not only accept but support our definition of TQM.

"Just like in manufacturing, the project's focus is on the customer, but our tools are designed to meet the needs of a project environment. The real strength of total quality as it applies to projects lies in its ability to increase our accuracy in predicting the likelihood of project success. Of course, you can reduce project cost, reduce the time to complete the project, and increase the assurance of meeting project specifications by using these techniques, too, but the real power lies in *the increase in project success*, because project success is directly tied to meeting the client's expectations."

John was watching the audience's reaction closely. They seemed a little confused but nobody was going to sleep. Feeling confident, he decided it was time to pick up the pace.

"LET'S LOOK AT SOME MYTHS that have grown up around the implementation of TQM. One myth that's bound to turn off project managers is that it takes a long time to implement TQM. If that were true, we could not implement TQM on projects at all, because we don't have a long time. That's the nature of a project. The reality is that you can start reaping benefits right away if you start off your project with a focusing workshop. Total Quality Management is not a big bang, but a constant stream of activities that harvest fruit for everybody involved in your project. Once you are focused on the concepts, the time you take to listen a little more carefully or to say 'thank you' will impact your project. You will not achieve everything you want, but you can have success from the outset.

"A second myth we hear constantly is that you cannot implement TQM without top management involvement. This may be true if we consider the project manager as the top management, but project managers in this company don't need any kind of blessing from top management to implement TQM on their projects. When division managers came to our project and said they liked what they saw, it encouraged the entire project team to take on more risk and reinforced our efforts. But even without this support we were enjoying success and would have had a client-focused, goal-directed, and people-oriented project anyway.

"You may hear, especially from our clients, that you need to do a great deal of TQM training to implement TQM on projects. But you can implement most of what we did on my project without any special training. The focusing workshop needed only the special facilitation skills of Ken Troy. We designed a process for developing and tracking goals. Celebrating and reinforcing successful achievement of those goals was a product of the management team's creativity. Focusing on the client and our orientation toward the team were principles developed *by the team*. The one exception where training was key was in the use of quality teams. Ken spent time teaching work process improvement skills to teams; skills like flow charting, brainstorming, problem analysis. With the exception of the quality teams, a project manager can create a total quality project without a quality training program."

John paused a moment to let that sink in. He wanted the audience to really hear that there was nothing stopping them from implementing TQM on their projects, that there were no prerequisites, and that implementation of TQM on projects was the function of *project management,* not top management or trained team members. Then he continued.

"Let's get down to the nitty-gritty. For a project to successfully implement Total Quality Management, it must be client-focused, goal-directed, and people-oriented. Are these concepts 'magic' that transform a project into an accomplishment? Or do these concepts keep consultants in business and do little else?

"To answer that, I'll tell a story. A couple of weeks ago, I was talking with a friend who has a project out of the Toronto office. During our conversation, he asked me, 'What was the secret to the success you had on your project?' I responded that the project was client-focused, goal-directed, and people-oriented. He looked me straight in the eye and said, 'Those are just buzzwords; they don't have any real meaning.'

"I was horrified; my project credo was holy to me! This guy just didn't understand. I was giving him the basis of a TQM project. Why ask me what's important if you're not going to listen?

"Then I remembered: Lesson Number One of a people-oriented project is to listen carefully; the more someone's statements bother you, the closer you should listen. So I said, in my most serious voice, 'Tell me more about what you're thinking.'

"Very shortly I understood that my friend was right, in his way. These *are* buzzwords that sometimes evoke a great deal of emotion, but mean nothing *until your project team puts meaning into them*.

"What meaning did our team give the words, *client-focused, goal-directed, and people-oriented*?

"*Client-focused* meant making decisions as if I were the client. It meant understanding the client's needs, concerns, and how this project fits into a larger business strategy. Our goal is to be a partner in a project that fulfills its strategic purpose. We do this by listening very carefully to the client, by mutually defining project success with the client, and by clearly defining roles and responsibilities, as well as by aligning project goals with the client's business needs. I also think it's important to identify key elements of success and develop a mechanism for tracking progress against these elements. One way to track softer issues, like communication, is to develop a client survey that asks the client to tell us how we are doing in these areas.

"To be truly client-focused, everybody on the project team must understand that we'll never do anything that breaches trust with a client. I believe you can do everything else right, but if you are not successful in building trust, the rest doesn't really matter. That trust comes from demonstrating competence, from being open and honest about our problems and vulnerabilities, and from giving the client honest feedback. Just as we need their feedback to adjust and improve, clients need our feedback to increase their contribution to the project's success.

"If I were asked to name the Number One contributor to project success, without hesitating, I would proclaim that *making decisions as if you were the client* is the core of the client-centered project. To do this you must listen, and listen with skill.

"Let me tell another story to emphasize this point. We were in a meeting with the client, the kind with five or six members from both staffs, trying to wrestle a sticky issue to the ground, when the client says to me, 'John, you're not hearing me.' I spent a good deal of the next hour trying to get the client to understand that I was hearing him just fine, but he just didn't understand the issue!"

John paused to let the audience indulge in a round of knowing chuckles. Then he continued, "We eventually came to consensus on a direction, but it was a tough meeting and we left without that sense of commitment you like to have when you're undertaking a difficult task.

"After the meeting, Ken Troy, our project process facilitator, took me aside and offered me some advice, which I now offer you free of charge. Whenever a person says 'you are not hearing me,' stop everything, push the emergency stop button, and focus on what that person's saying. Repeat back to him what you *think* he is saying and ask for confirmation. The most important words in the project manager's vocabulary are, 'I hear you saying ...' Keep asking how close you are until there's agreement that you really do understand.

"Once a person believes you don't understand, nothing else is relevant. He or she is no longer part of the process if there's no effort to understand what's going on. You lose that person's contribution. By stopping and focusing on understanding, you help the group focus, you take yourself out of the role of defending your position and you become a builder of consensus. By listening, the team stops trying to build better arguments for their position while others are talking. Instead, they encourage building a better decision by taking the best ideas from each team member. I strongly recommend that you develop that 'emergency stop button' that automatically reacts when you hear the words, 'you're not hearing me.'

"A *goal-directed* project has two points of focus: developing the right goals and making sure that activities are focused on goals and not goals focused on activities. Once the project establishes a vision of success and defines critical goals to achieve that success, goals will cascade throughout the project, flowing from the project management team, through each function, to each team member on the project. On our project, each individual was encouraged to have three goals each week, and to know how these goals contributed to the success of the team. Individual goals were tied to the function and functional goals were tied to the project.

"Because projects are one-time occurrences, the goal development process is needed to tie the project's organization together. Developing and tracking goals provides a means of communicating what's important and helps the project team know how they are doing against the plan. If goals are mutually developed, the goal development process also communicates to team members that they are partners and fellow problem solvers on this project.

"Goals also provide one other important function. They provide a natural opportunity to celebrate, to recognize the team's success during the life of the project, and allow the team to build on that success.

"Now, I don't think this focus on goals would be very popular with the TQM professionals of the manufacturing environment. When I searched Dr. Deming's book, *Out of the Crisis,* I found only two references to goals in the index of a 492-page book. Deming's focus is on the work *process*. If a manager focuses on improving the process, then the organization will achieve its goals. Goals, in this environment, can get in the way of improvement because people will manipulate the process to achieve the goal, not necessarily to improve the process.

"Now, I'm not arguing that focusing on processes is *wrong*. What I am saying is that project management must develop tools, techniques and processes appropriate to the *project* environment. Our needs, the skills we apply, and the processes we use are necessarily different than in a continuous-process organization. We cannot uncritically adopt quality concepts that work in that environment and expect them to work the same way on a project.

"Finally, here's the difficult one: *people-oriented*. On some projects you can feel the excitement, the sense of urgency, and the commitment. On others you feel friction and frustration. What accounts for this difference? Although a lot of outside influences affect project morale, I believe that we as project managers have the biggest influence on the morale of our project. If you believe as I do, that this morale has a significant impact on a project, then we should be spending an equally significant portion of our time and energy creating that healthy project environment.

"We could spend hours on this topic, looking at the use of reinforcement, communication, celebrations, and other people issues. Instead, allow me to leave you with one observation. People on projects have a certain spirit in their eyes when they identify with the vision of

157

success, believe that they impact that success, and know they will be recognized for their contribution. The worst thing you can say is 'that's *your* job.' It's more than a job. It's a partnering, and we have a responsibility as project managers to find a way to make everybody who works on our project a partner.

"Challenge people, ask them for their ideas, and encourage them to be innovative in their contributions. Above all, respect people—it will show in everything we do.

"To quote John Nesbitt, from *Reinventing the Corporation*, 'When you identify with your company's purpose, when you experience ownership of a shared vision, you find yourself doing your life's work instead of doing time.' I do work that is meaningful to me. I have received recognition for success. I have found balance in my work. Sometimes it's very enjoyable and relaxing, and sometimes hard and challenging. I have found balance with other aspects of my life, too, and most of all I'm having fun.

"I WANT TO LEAVE YOU with a challenge. You have an obligation to your company and to your profession to explore new ways of implementing Total Quality Management on your projects. Mold it to your project and your needs. Improve the processes and share your learnings. Project management has a large role to play in the continued evolution of the world economy, and we had better make some quantum leaps in the way we manage projects or we will become the dinosaurs of the management world.

"I remember bragging one day about how our project team had found *the answer*. If we could just duplicate the secrets we'd discovered on our project, we could make a major shift in the way our company does business. Ken Troy gently reminded me that if we perfectly duplicated the experience we'd just finished, we would fall behind— because part of the secret lies in always striving to do better. Our discoveries are just the beginning, and I invite you to join the journey."

The applause erupted as John said his thank-yous, and grew as he hugged Judy before he took his seat again. The audience began to rise and the applause grew louder. John had never experienced anything like this; he was a little embarrassed but he enjoyed the warmth of the response. He hoped that Ken, Lucy, Andre, Geoff, Danny, and all the others who had helped create this moment could feel pride in what they had accomplished. Most had already moved on to their next project, trying to build on their team experience together. He looked back fondly on the work they had done together, and wondered for a moment if he would ever top this experience.

Then he looked ahead and smiled to himself in anticipation, because he knew that every project, every team, could create its own unique magic.

To do what you love and feel that it matters—what could be more fun?
Katherine Graham, publisher of the Washington Post

Appendix A: A Brief Overview of Project Management Concepts

Project Management: The application of knowledge, skills, tools, and techniques to project activities in order to meet or exceed stakeholder needs and expectations ...

This is the definition of project management found in the Project Management Institute's *A Guide to the Project Management Body of Knowledge* (1996). Sounds simple, but for most project managers the correct application of those skills, tools and techniques entails a lifetime of experiences and learning.

A project manager transforms someone's dream into a reality. She translates a raw concept into a deliverable, builds an organization and structure to produce that deliverable, and then decommissions that organization. It is the temporary nature of this organization that gives rise to the special character of a project, a character that is very different from that of an ongoing organization. The character of a project organization defines the skills, the knowledge and the management approach that is needed to be successful.

Projects have identifiable phases and each phase has a unique set a challenges for the project manager. During the *Initiation* phase, the project deliverables are defined and the resources needed to execute the project are identified. The project manager launches the organization and articulates his vision of project success.

During the *Planning* phase, the project vision is translated into a detailed plan to produce each of the project deliverables. Project tasks are identified and resources are allocated to the deliverables. The project manager provides the framework to balance the project's need for structure, while creating a culture that encourages and supports the appropriate level of empowerment.

During the *Production* (or *Execution*) phase, the project team executes the plan, tracking progress against the plan, monitoring and controlling progress against the allocation of resources and time. The project manager ensures that current information is provided to various managers of the project to control their progress, while encouraging an environment of creative problem-solving.

During the project's *Close-out* phase, project deliverables are fine-tuned to meet the requirements of the project's customer. (This also takes place during the start-up phases; in fact, the more effectively this is done at start-up, the less traumatic closeout becomes ... hence the importance of applying TQM on projects!) During close-out, project resources are reallocated and the project organization shuts down. The project manager maintains the project focus on the customer's requirements and the project's energy level, while assisting the smooth transition of resources from inside the project to outside.

Project managers must create an organization, nurture it through its various stages of development and then dissolve the organization. The project manager creates the project culture, understands and manages the project technology, aligns the project team toward a common goals, establishes the appropriate project infrastructure, provides persuasive leadership, applies effective management skills and techniques, and generates enthusiasm.

Appendix B: A Brief Overview of Quality Concepts

Productivity is the main ingredient needed for an increased standard of living in any society. It also provides a competitive advantage for a product in the marketplace. The United States' transformation to an industrial economy can be attributed largely to the increases in productivity brought about by advances in farming techniques such as Eli Whitney's cotton gin and Cyrus McCormick's reaper. In the same way, the Japanese industrial strength of the '70s reflected their higher productivity rates in key industries such as automobile manufacturing.

In response to the growing Japanese competitive challenge, in the 1970s and '80s the business management focus on increasing productivity shifted from a reliance on *physical* capital investment to *human* capital investment. As advanced industrial economies shifted to what Alvin Toffler labeled "the Third Wave" and Richard Crawford called "the Knowledge Economy," investment also shifted from machines to people. In the 1940s less than 5 percent of the U.S. population over the age of 25 had attended college. By 1989, over half of Americans aged eighteen had started college. The average school years completed went from eight to over twelve years. In the 1950s, direct expenditure on physical capital was twice the expenditure on education. But by 1988, that trend had reversed and is still changing.

This focus on human capital has led to new techniques in management. It was found that those management techniques that had successfully produced maximum output from machines actually *decreased* production when applied to production that required human investment and creativity. Techniques that focused on human capital emerged.

As our understanding of human motivation and workplace culture increased, work process improvement skills and techniques were developed. "Our employees are our great asset" and "our only assets leave in the elevator every night" became slogans that represented this new emphasis on human capital.

Quality circles, self-directed work teams, work process improvement, Continuous Performance Improvement, 360-degree evaluations, empowerment, customer-driven improvement, focus on customer satisfaction, reengineering, and value-driven cultures all reflect a focus on the human capital investment. These investments have made significant improvements in productivity, which allows a larger investment in human capital, which produces better productivity...

163

TQM is a label. It labels this investment in human capital and the focus on productivity improvement, whether it be in work processes or cultural enhancements. As important segments of our economy shift from a machine-based capital formation to human-based capital, new management techniques to enhance this investment will continue to develop. Even new technological developments must be applied in a new work environment. The understanding and application of TQM will evolve with these new management techniques. TQM has changed significantly from its early focus on quality control to a focus on empowerment and reengineering. It will continue to change as the management environment in which TQM is applied changes.

Appendix C: Theory X-Theory Y Management

Management theorist Douglas McGregor developed "Theory X" and "Theory Y" to describe two sets of assumptions that influence the behavior of managers towards their subordinates.

The "Theory X" manager operates under the assumption that most employees dislike their work and will try to avoid it. According to these managers, people lack ambition and have little talent for problem solving and creativity; they prefer to be directed and managed, rather than taking responsibility or initiative. The Theory X employee is self-centered, indifferent to organizational needs and resistant to change; he or she is motivated only by lower-level needs such as job security, workplace safety, and dependable compensation (salary and benefits). The typical Theory X employee follows the path of least resistance instead of trying to suggest changes and is motivated solely by money and/or threat of punishment.

Naturally, managers who hold these assumptions tend to be rigid, authoritarian and suspicious. Their organizations are characterized by strict rules and policies and tight supervisory control. Unfortunately, this creates a self-fulfilling prophecy: if you believe workers are incapable of creativity and responsibility, you set up a structure that makes it impossible for them to show their creativity or assume responsibility—thus effectively weeding out the most creative and responsible individuals and "dumbing down" the organization.

Theory Y managers, on the other hand, are supportive managers. They believe that most employees will meet high performance expectations if they are given the appropriate motivators, including a supportive work climate. Such managers expect people to be creative, ambitious and committed to organizational goals. They take for granted that their subordinates have self-discipline and can direct and control their own activities—in fact, that they desire and will actively seek ways to take responsibility. Such employees are motivated by money, of course—but also by their interest in the work itself and the intrinsic rewards that performing it well bring them, such as the esteem of their peers and recognition for accomplishments.

Theory Y managers develop a hands-off approach to management. Organizations are more loosely structured and decision making is participatory. They emphasize opportunities for development and growth.

In the project environment—especially in application areas such as new product development, architecture, publishing, marketing, etc., where the majority of team members are highly-skilled, educated "knowledge workers"— Theory Y management is generally acknowledged to produce better outcomes.

For more discussion of this topic, see McGregor's *The Human Side of Enterprise*, McGraw-Hill, 1985; or Vijay Verma's *Human Resource Skills for the Project Manager*, Project Management Institute, 1996.

Appendix D: Stages of Team Development

Volumes have been written about how to develop, manage and nurture teams. The stages of development that Ken is talking about, however, were theorized and named by management researchers Hersey and Blanchard (*Management of Organizational Behavior: Utilizing Human Resources*, Prentice Hall, 1988), who identified four developmental stages in the maturation of a team—much like the developmental stages an individual passes through as he or she matures into an adult. Those stages are:

1. **Forming**. The team comes together for their initial meetings. Members are polite, businesslike and guarded about their true thoughts and feelings. Icebreakers and team building exercises can help forge unity during this stage.

2. **Storming**. The gloves come off. Team members confront each other and struggle for position and control. Dissenters can either be accepted as a valuable source of input at this point or they will opt out, either by leaving the team or by refusing to fully participate.

3. **Norming**. The team begins to come together, confronting issues instead of people. They establish procedures, learn to make decisions collectively, and individual members become team-oriented.

4. **Performing**. With personal, power, and procedural issues out of the way, the team gets down to business, putting forth productive effort in an atmosphere of trust, flexibility, and cohesiveness. A team that successfully reaches this stage is, of course, quite capable of self-direction.

Naturally, on a time-limited project, all these developmental stages must be successfully gotten through in a much shorter time frame. This is the critical difference and challenge of team management on projects that Ken refers to in Chapter 7.

Book Three of PMI's Human Aspects of Project Management Series, *Managing the Project Team*, by Vijay K. Verma (1996) gives a good overview of team management theory and practice.

Appendix E: The Meyers-Briggs Type Indicator

The MBTI was developed in the 1940s by Katherine Briggs and her daughter, Isabel Briggs-Meyers, psychologists who were interested in developing practical applications of Swiss psychologist Carl Jung's work on personality assessment. Psychologists and human-resource specialists who are trained and certified in the use of the MBTI find that it can be useful in vocational or educational counseling, placement in business or industry, and as a tool in workshops and seminars designed to help people who work or live together better understand one another and resolve conflicts.

The MBTI is a set of 126 to 166 (depending on the form of the test used) questions, which are easily answered in under an hour. One set of items asks how one actually feels or acts in a given situation; the other asks the participant to choose the preferred word in a pair. The resulting scores measure where the individual falls on four indices of personality characteristics:

- **Extraversion-Intraversion** (E or I) reflects whether a person directs their attention mainly to the outer world of people and things or mainly toward the inner world of ideas.
- **Sensing-Intuition** (S or N) reflects which kind of perception—that based on concrete observations of the senses, or that based on insight, possibilities and imagination—the person most relies on.
- **Thinking-Feeling** (T or F) reflects which kind of judgment the person most trusts when a decision needs to be made—that based on analysis and logic, or that based on personal values.
- **Judgment-Perception** (J or P) reflects whether the person prefers to deal with the world from a judging attitude (evaluating, planning, coming to conclusions) or a perceptive attitude (information gathering, seeking inspiration, relying on spontaneity).

The combination of the four indices yields a possible sixteen personality types, expressed as four letters: INFJ or ESTP, for example. The value of the Meyers Briggs score is that it is nonjudgmental—there are no "good" or "bad" personality types. As descriptions of preferred ways of perceiving, interacting and making decisions, the types merely communicate to others essential information about how an individual looks at the world, processes information, and chooses to relate to others—valuable input in any personal or work relationship.

The nonprofit Center for Applications of Psychological Type in Gainesville, Florida is the premier source for information on the use of the MBTI. Today, in addition to the long form of the evaluation which must be administered by a certified professional, there are self-administered forms that can be computer-scored with software from the CAPT. However, to truly understand and get the most benefit from the MBTI, it helps to have some background in psychology and an acquaintance with Jung's theories as well as the body of research findings on how the MBTI scores can be interpreted and put to use.

Appendix F: The "Lifeline" Exercise

This exercise, which Lucy refers to in Chapter 9, is a popular icebreaker at team building and organizational development meetings. The materials are simple: large sheets of paper (flip chart sheets work well), enough colored markers for everyone to have a selection, and tables roomy enough for each participant to have a work area.

Each participant draws a "Lifeline:" a time line beginning with his or her birth and extending to the present. On the Lifeline they are asked to mark and explain in a few words key events in their personal and/or professional development: when they realized they wanted a career in their chosen field; starting college, receiving a degree; meaningful work experiences (positive or negative); marriage, the birth of a child, and so on. The contents of the Lifeline can be strictly work-related, or they may be deeply personal, depending the group and the individual.

Some individuals Lifelines will be simple and factual: a straight line with a few key events pinpointed; others will be wildly colorful, incorporate idiosyncratic events of deep personal meaning, wind all over the page like a country road, or illustrate key events with drawings. The individuality of the process is part of its value in helping team members get to know each other better, not only their histories but their work styles.

Participants can then be invited to extend the Lifeline into the future and map out their aspirations and expectations for the future.

Sharing these "life maps" with each other in a workshop or retreat setting is an excellent way to help team members realize their commonalities and appreciate their differences. It also marks the current project as an important event in each individual's life story.

Appendix G: Reflective Listening

Listening is a vastly underrated communication skill. Usually, when we think of good communication, we focus on the output side of the process: the spoken or written word, the effective use of images. But communication doesn't take place unless the message is properly received, and for that to occur, the audience must be *listening*.

Merely hearing the words that someone says isn't the same as good listening. The good listener evaluates the entire content of the message: tone of voice, body language, and underlying emotional content to fully understand what the speaker is saying. One way to be sure the message you receive is the same one the sender intended to send is to utilize reflective listening techniques, as John does in Chapter 10.

Reflective listening is a time-honored technique in the helping professions. Counselors, for whom effective listening is the stock-in-trade, rely on it to establish relationships with clients, verify their perceptions of what a client is saying, and help clients "hear themselves"—get a more objective view of their own concerns. It works, and this is how it works:

1. Establish a communication-friendly environment. Reduce distractions; close the office door, put aside papers and other things that may distract your attention. Use body language to show you are listening: lean forward, make eye contact, and stop talking.

2. Listen "between the lines:" make note of the emotions that seem to underlie the words. For example, when a team member says, "If she wants to do my job as well as hers, that's okay by me," does he mean that literally? Or do the words mask resentment and frustration?

3. Summarize your understanding of the situation periodically, including the emotional content. "Let me see if I understand. You had the task planned but when you set your plan in motion, you discovered that Ellen had already assigned someone else to do it in a different way. You sound angry about that—am I right?"

4. If the speaker has a general gripe—"He's always sticking his nose in my business,"—ask for specific examples.

5. If the speaker makes a wild assertion, repeat it back to him. "Ellen is out to get me!"

"So, you think that Ellen is consciously trying to discredit you."

Sometimes when we hear what we actually said, we realize that is overstated, even irrational. Just having our statements repeated back to us in a dispassionate manner can sometimes show us what is inappropriate in our own thought patterns or behavior.

6. Direct the speaker to the most appropriate listener, as John does in Chapter 10 when he suggests that Geoff talk over the situation that made him angry with Danny, instead of going over his head. Try to make a plan with the speaker so that he or she can solve the problem—don't make the problem your own.

For an excellent overview of communication skills, including listening skills, see Vijay Verma's *Human Resource Skills for Project Managers,* Project Management Institute, 1996.

Appendix H: Suggested Reading

Adams, Scott. 1996. *The Dilbert Principle,* and *Dogbert's Top Secret Management Handbook.*

Barker, Joel Arthur. 1996. *Discovering the Future: The Business of Paradigms.* St. Paul, Minn.:ILI Press.

Bennis, Warren and Robert Townsend. 1995. *Reinventing Leadership.* New York: William Morrow and Company.

Crawford, Richard. 1991. *In The Era of Human Capital.* Harper Business.

Fromm, Erich. 1945. *Escape from Freedom.* Holt, Rinehart and Winston.

Hobson, J. Allan, M.D. 1994. *The Chemistry of Conscious States: How the Brain Changes its Mind.* New York: Little, Brown and Company.

House, Ruth Sizemore. 1988. *The Human Side of Project Management.* Addison-Wesley.

Key Ideas in Human Thought. 1993. Edited by Kenneth McLeish. New York: Facts on File, Inc.

Khadem, Riaz and Robert Lorber. 1996. *One Page Management.* New York: Quill William Morrow.

Peters, Tom. *In Search of Excellence, Thriving on Chaos, The Pursuit of Wow.*

Pirsig, Robert M. 1974. *Zen and the Art of Motorcycle Maintenance: An Inquiry into Values.* William Morrow.

PMI Standards Committee. 1996. *A Guide to the Project Management Body of Knowledge.* Upper Darby, Penn.: Project Management Institute.

Roberts, Wes and Bill Ross. 1995. *Make It So: Leadership Lessons from Star Trek.* Pocket Books.

Schaffer, Robert H. 1988. *The Breakthrough Strategy.* Harper Business.

Swets, Paul W. 1983. *The Art of Talking so that People Will Listen.* New York: Prentice Hall Press.

Toffler, Alvin. *Powershift* (1990) , *Future Shock* (1970), *The Third Wave.*

Verma, Vijay K. 1996. *Human Resource Skills for the Project Manager.* Upper Darby, Penn.: Project Management Institute. Also, Volume Three of the same series, *Managing the Project Team* (1996).

Wheatley, Margaret J. 1994. *Leadership and the New Science: Learning about Organization from an Orderly Universe.* San Francisco, Calif.: Berrett-Koehler.